STRESS
IN MINISTRY
CAUSES AND CURES

ERNEST DIXON MURRAH, JR.

WESTBOW
PRESS®
A DIVISION OF THOMAS NELSON
& ZONDERVAN

Scripture quoted from the King James Version of the Bible.

WestBow Press books may be ordered through booksellers or by contacting:

WestBow Press
A Division of Thomas Nelson & Zondervan
1663 Liberty Drive
Bloomington, IN 47403
www.westbowpress.com
1 (866) 928-1240

ISBN: 978-1-5127-7770-3 (sc)
ISBN: 978-1-5127-7771-0 (hc)
ISBN: 978-1-5127-7769-7 (e)

Library of Congress Control Number: 2017905592

Print information available on the last page.

WestBow Press rev. date: 06/13/2017

CONTENTS

PREFACE

THIS BOOK IS designed as a mentoring guide for ministry. It is presented in an informal style for the common pastor or layman rather than for the academia. The material is straight to the point and may even be offensive or strong to some readers, but it is written that way for emphasis and for the purpose of impacting the reader in a more personal way. It is our prayer that this book will be a valuable resource to those in ministry as they face the stresses and conflicts that ministry will most certainly bring.

The number of ministers who leave the ministry each year due to stress and burnout is appalling. This exodus is not limited to just one denomination, but in some denominations, more ministers are leaving the ministry each year than the number of those preparing to enter it. Church conflicts are occurring more frequently and with more devastating effects.

Recent research by US Films indicates that church fights impact every denomination of Christianity in America. Sadly, more clergy are leaving the ministry now than ever before, and many times it is the result of conflict. Unfortunately, most clergy have had no training in dealing with conflict (US Films, *Betrayed: Clergy Killer*).

Since 1984, Lifeway of the Southern Baptist Convention has been collecting data through the pastoral ministries division of each state's convention to determine how many pastors are being terminated from their churches each year. Approximately two hundred pastors are fired every month (Donald Q. Hicks). In an effort to reduce that number and to bring some resolution to this ever-increasing problem in ministry, this work has been penned. After nearly a quarter of a century of counseling with more than one thousand couples in ministry from six countries and across twenty different denominations, my wife and I have discovered the following major areas of concern that impact the physical, emotional, and spiritual health of most ministers. These areas of concern are not listed in any particular order, but every problem encountered usually falls into one of them.

Our primary goal in dispensing this information is to glorify God, along with the secondary objective of preparing a tool that will aid those in ministry to not only to think critically but to accept the Bible as the inerrant, infallible, and all-sufficient guide for practical ministry. This work has also been designed specifically with counsel for the minister, clergy, or pastor in mind. With regard to developing a pattern of critical thinking, it is imperative that the minister be able to research and carefully evaluate various concepts and ideas before totally incorporating them into life and ministry. It will be shown in this work how the educational system is no longer concerned with teaching logic or critical thinking, and as a result the foundations of society are in disarray and decay.

We have a hope for the future, but this hope and the remedies for the numerous challenges of service in the church cannot be resolved without considering how to answer these questions in light of God's Word. As we look into these areas of concern, we will attempt to give biblical counsel on how to handle each one. Too often, many younger ministers place a heavy reliance on their natural gifts, developed abilities, and acquired educational accomplishments for their ministry. This approach can lead to disastrous results without godly counsel and insightful mentoring from those who have learned to deal with the stress and constant struggles of the plight of the pastor, clergy, or minister.

ACKNOWLEDGMENTS

IN THE WRITING of this book, I have learned a lot. For one thing, I learned how some of our grandchildren feel about me and my writing. Our oldest grandson told his dad, our oldest son, "Dad, remember that Granddad is a scientist and not a writer." I guess that is why I have needed the help of so many people in preparing this book.

Several years ago, Dr. Martin Sanders told me that I should write this book. The Bible says that in the mouth of two witnesses, a thing is so. When Dr. Denny Autry suggested the same thing, and I said, "There is the second witness," so I began the book. Dr. Autry and his staff made a number of very valuable suggestions and other input. I can't thank him enough.

My dear wife's encouragement and input have been no small factor in its preparation. Lois is thankful for this book because I always told her after I died, this would be her project. She has shared in my graduate studies and ministry, so she had a very large part in generating the material in the book. Special thanks go to my lovely wife, without whose help, encouragement, and understanding I could not have written this book.

I am thankful for all the counseling clients and the Stress in the Ministry conference participants for sharing their stories with me; their contribution allows me to give back to others some of what I have learned.

Many people have had a profound influence on my life and ministry, many of which I do not remember their names. Some of the names that I do remember are B. O. Harrell, Hank Bryan, Dr. Kenneth Wetcher, Goldie Rappaport, Dr. Uri Ruvenie, Dr. Jim Mahoney, Vendyl Jones, and Dr. John D. Morgan. Many books and their authors have also helped.

Some of the folks who were of a major help in editing this book were Michele Hurst, Dr. Denny Autry, Jeffrey Murrah, Damon Murrah, Cathy Edwards, and Dr. Steve Silverstein.

This book and the ministry that produced the Stress in the Ministry conferences were made possible by the original idea and suggestion of Dr. John Morgan, pastor of Sagemont Church. Total funding of the weeklong conferences was supplied by Hank and Darlene Bryan for some fifteen or more years. The last few years' funding came from Sagemont Church. The conferences originally began as a joint effort between Sagemont Church and RAPHA. Dr. Jim Mahoney of RAPHA was my co-leader for the first year, and then RAPHA dropped out due to the death of Dr. Mahoney.

CHAPTER 1

DEFINING MINISTRY IN THE CONTEMPORARY CHURCH

IN ORDER TO define ministry in the contemporary church, it is imperative to do some self-evaluation. Before I begin any counseling session, whether is it a layman, minister, or pastor, it is important to ask some foundational questions. "Are you a Christian? How do you know? Have you ever confessed your sins and asked Jesus to save you?" Salvation does not stem from one being raised in a Christian family, or having gone to church all his or her life, or having been baptized or from doing good deeds, or a lot of other things. It only comes through trusting in and obeying Jesus.

The next question to consider is, "Are you called of God to the responsibility of ministry?" Many go into the vocational ministry without truly being called by God. We can be called by our parents, especially if they were in the ministry. Sigmund Freud found that many men go into the ministry to try to escape the temptations of this world. Still others find the appeal of the attention, stage, and spotlight very attractive. The Bible says that every Christian is to do ministry (Eph. 4:11), but that does not mean everyone is called into the profession of vocational ministry.

> For the *perfecting of the saints, for the work of the ministry*, for the edifying of the body of Christ. (Ephesians 4:12)[1]

When asked by a young person about going into the ministry, I tell them that if they can do anything other than going into ministry, they should do it. Ministry, as a profession or vocation, is one of the most difficult and stressful areas of service in which a person can work. Other questions need to be asked regarding ministry include, "Why do you want to go into the ministry? Have you really evaluated your reasons? What is your true motivation? Are you being totally honest?" Some specific questions to ask are, "Do I have a fervent desire to teach, or preach, or lead music? Do I have any special gifts that would help me minister effectively? Do I truly love God and His word? Do I feel like I must be in the ministry or die? Am I willing to sacrifice all that I have to be in the ministry?"

Within the ministry are two types of calls: an inward call and an outward call. The inner call is the most important and has been expressed by some as "God's voice heard by faith" (Martin Luther), or as "an intense, all-absorbing desire for the work" (Charles H. Spurgeon). This inward calling is all about serving Christ and

---

[1] All scripture is from the King James Version unless otherwise noted. Also, any italics in quotations are my own added emphasis.

helping others. It is not about any self-serving goals or agendas. The outward call is from a church or group that asks you to minister to them. Here again, one must be careful in considering this type of call. "Is it of truly God? How do I know?" Sometimes a church or group will want you for appearance's sake or some other reason. You might even feel tempted to accept an outward calling because it pays more, has a larger congregation, is closer to home, or has some other emotional attraction.

Once the question as to one's calling to Christian service has been settled, then must one must consider, "What is church ministry?" Many tend to think it is self-evident as to what church ministry really means. The accurate definition of church ministry is probably best defined by God as stated in Matthew 22:37–39. "Jesus said unto him, 'Thou shalt love the Lord thy God with all thy heart, and with all thy soul, and with all thy mind. This is the first and great commandment. And the second is like unto it, Thou shalt love thy neighbour as thyself.'" The practical application of this definition can be found in Matthew 28:19–20. "Go ye therefore, and teach all nations, baptizing them in the name of the Father, and of the Son, and of the Holy Ghost: Teaching them to observe all things whatsoever I have commanded you: and, lo, I am with you always, even unto the end of the world. Amen." The only way we can teach anyone anything is by example, and that means we have to set the example of obeying Christ in all aspects of our lives so that others can follow our example and thus glorify God. One very important self-evaluation is, "Do you love yourself?" If you do not love yourself, how can you truly love Christ because the "real you" is already just like Christ?

> Herein is our love made perfect, that we may have boldness in the day of judgment: because *as he is, so are we in this world.* (1 John 4:17)

> Honour thy father and thy mother: and, *Thou shalt love thy neighbour as thyself.* (Matt. 19:19)

> And the second is like unto it, *Thou shalt love thy neighbour as thyself.* (Matt. 22:39).

If you do not love yourself, you cannot (do not) truly love others. Remember that love as God defines it and demonstrates it is not an emotion per se; it is an action reflected through one's behavior and obedience.

> If ye love me, keep my commandments. (John 14:15)

So what should ministry look like? The best example can be found by looking at how the early church ministered in biblical times. We can find examples in Ephesians 4:12–15, Romans 12:15–17, and Acts 2:42–47. In these passages, ministry is exhibited by Bible teaching, living biblical teaching, engaging in fellowship with one another, eating together, helping those in need, showing love to everyone, and being a good witness for Christ in all activities.

> For the perfecting of the saints, for the work of the ministry, for the edifying of the body of Christ:

Till we all come in the unity of the faith, and of the knowledge of the Son of God, unto a perfect man, unto the measure of the stature of the fullness of Christ: That we henceforth be no more children, tossed to and fro, and carried about with every wind of doctrine, by the sleight of men, and cunning craftiness, whereby they lie in wait to deceive; But speaking the truth in love, may grow up into him in all things, which is the head, even Christ. (Eph. 4:12–15)

And they continued steadfastly in the apostles' doctrine and fellowship, and in breaking of bread, and in prayers. And fear came upon every soul: and many wonders and signs were done by the apostles. And all that believed were together, and had all things common; And sold their possessions and goods, and parted them to all men, as every man had need. And they, continuing daily with one accord in the temple, and breaking bread from house to house, did eat their meat with gladness and singleness of heart, Praising God, and having favour with all the people. And the Lord added to the church daily such as should be saved. (Acts 2:42–47)

Rejoice with them that do rejoice, and weep with them that weep. Be of the same mind one toward another. Mind not high things, but condescend to men of low estate. Be not wise in your own conceits. Recompense to no man evil for evil. Provide things honest in the sight of all men. (Rom. 12:15–17)

Often we want to decide what church ministry should be, but the church and its ministries belong to God and are to be done His way. Because it is God's ministry, we must have a philosophy of ministry that is in accordance with scripture. When we look at ministry through the lens of scripture, we become more effective, more fruitful, and more faithful to our call to ministry, which in turn helps the church to be what God intended and what God desires it to be. While doing all this, we need to keep in mind that God's plan is for the church to change the culture, and not the culture to change the church. The church is only "the church" when it operates God's way. Too many ministers let the culture influence the church in order to attract more people. This attempt to be culturally relevant can stem from pride or ignorance on the minister's part and not be what God truly wants.

> If any man think himself to be a prophet, or spiritual, let him acknowledge that the things that I write unto you are the commandments of the Lord. (1 Cor. 14:37)

A very important part of church ministry is the pulpit ministry, but it is only one part of the total ministry. Church ministry is also made up of music and other ministers, teachers, and laymen. I will be using the term *pastor* to reference any type of minister or ministry. As pastors, we must always keep in our minds and actions that our real power for ministry is the Holy Spirit! Regardless of which ministry one may be serving, the spotlight must be on Christ and not on oneself. A good question to keep in mind when ministering to an individual person or to a large crowd is, "Are they seeing Jesus or me?" God wants them to see Jesus at all times.

> And this is love, that we walk after his commandments. This is the commandment, That, as ye have heard from the beginning, ye should walk in it. (2 John 1:6)

CHAPTER 2

WHAT IS EXPECTED OF A MINISTER TODAY?

THE SIMPLEST AND most direct answer to what is expected of a minister today by God is that we do things God's way. Unfortunately, it is not what many churches want and expect from us in today's culture. Our culture wants to hear messages that make them feel good.

> For the time will come when they will not endure sound doctrine; but after their own lusts shall they heap to themselves teachers, having itching ears; And they shall turn away their ears from the truth, and shall be turned unto fables. (2 Tim. 4:3–4)

So what does God want in terms of messages and teachings? A short answer is found in 2 Timothy 4:2. "Preach the word; be instant in season, out of season; reprove, rebuke, exhort with all longsuffering and doctrine."

What God wants and expects from ministers is to preach and teach what He says in the Bible, whether or not it is politically correct. That includes admonishing those that need it, censuring those that need it (call sin for what it is), and encouraging believers to obey Christ and be good witnesses. We must not neglect lifting up Jesus and telling folks about the need for a personal savior, which can only be found in accepting Jesus Christ as their Lord and savior. That means trusting Him for their salvation and obeying Him out of love for Him. If we love Jesus, we will obey Him.

> If ye love me, keep my commandments. (John 14:15)

> He that hath my commandments, and keepeth them, he it is that loveth me: and he that loveth me shall be loved of my Father, and I will love him, and will manifest myself to him. (John 14:21)

> And hereby we do know that we know him, if we keep his commandments. 4 He that saith, I know him, and keepeth not his commandments, is a liar, and the truth is not in him. (1 John 2:3–4)

A really important concept to watch out for is perception. All of us have thought that we have seen or heard something, and then we found out that we were mistaken. Our five senses send information to our brains. Our brains then evaluate information and come up with some perception which may or may not be accurate and correct.

As you work with people you have to be very careful in your perception of them. To make a misperception could cause you a lot of stress. Do not jump to conclusions! Always carefully evaluate your perceptions.

CHAPTER 3

STRESS

IF ONE HOLDS himself up as a teacher or leader and an example of how to best to live life, that person had better walk the walk. Nowhere is that more important than in the ministry.

Some critical areas of emotions that are of special importance to us ministers are stress and burnout. We will begin by exploring stress, and later in the book, we can examine the effects of burnout. We will refer to the minister/pastor and the church/ministry interchangeably. How ministers handle stress is of primary importance as we live our lives in front of our families and those to whom we minister.

People often talk about how much stress they are under. Ministers are no exception; if anything, we are probably under more real stressors than many other folks. Most people in our culture believe that if people are not stressed out, they must not have enough to do. A Southern Baptist article published in 2004 states that stress and stress-related issues are the number one medical problem among

Southern Baptist ministers. Long-term stress adversely affects both the brain and the body.

What is stress? Stress really is a cover-up word for worry, fear, or anger. Think about how many times the Bible tells us not to worry. Why? Because God wants us to trust Him and His plans for our lives. We are taught in our culture to worry from an early age. How often did we hear our parents and others tell us to be careful? We often say to others that they should "be safe" or "drive carefully." What is the hidden but plain message in these sayings? The underlying message is really telling us to worry that something might happen to us.

Just what is stress? Stress is the result of one or more stressors. A stressor (a person, place, event, or incident) is anything, whether positive or negative, that puts pressure on us. It can be something positive like marriage, the first child, or a promotion. A negative stressor can be something like a death, job loss, marital problems, or divorce. "Physiological stress is not the outside pressure of the impacting force on a person but the body's own response to that pressure" (E. H. Friedman). In the same way, emotional stress is not what is going on around us, but it is our own emotional reaction to the situation. Albert Einstein is quoted as saying, "Problems cannot be solved at the same level of awareness that created them." If we do not increase our awareness and understanding of what stress and its accompanying frustration is about (and often resentment too), we will not be able to resolve the situation. Most of life occurs in a cycle of cause and effect.

"Stress is a signal that something needs to change. What we call stress is really just a series of chemical reactions in our brain and body" (Bill Crawford, *The Top of the Mind*). As a general rule, these chemical reactions help us be productive unless they increase to the point where we become less or unproductive. The primary chemical reaction of stress, sometimes referred to as fight or flight syndrome, is the production of adrenalin and cortisol. When we are stressed for an extended period of time, the body's production of cortisol releases extra glucose (sugar), which usually turns into fat. It also stops the production of protein, which results in fewer white blood cells and can ultimately lead to a weakened immune system. The adrenalin shuts down the stomach, causing shifts in blood concentration within the body, which results in shallow breathing and causing the capillaries near the surface of the skin to retreat deeper into the body.

That reaction can have a positive or negative affect depending upon the kind of image we are thinking about, and on which we are holding in our minds. That is one reason that God wants us to think positively.

> Finally, brethren, whatsoever things are true, whatsoever things are honest, whatsoever things are just, whatsoever things are pure, whatsoever things are lovely, whatsoever things are of good report; if

there be any virtue, and if there be any praise, think
on these things. (Phil. 4:8)

Now that we understand what stress is and what it can do to our
physical bodies, we will examine what common stressors are for one
in the ministry. Life, and especially the Christian life, is all about
relationships. We are part of three families: our family of origin, our
marriage and current family, and our church family. A problem in
any one of our families will show up as problems in our other two
families. If our family is suffering, the church is suffering, and vice
versa. An old truism is, "The pew always reflects the pulpit."

One common stress factor for ministers is that of growing
one's ministry. Many ministers think that ministry growth is their
responsibility. Numerical growth is God's job, not ours. Our job is
to equip the people for the work of the ministry and to set the right
example for them, which is how we love and disciple them. Many
churches will try to tell us that numerical growth is our job, but we
have to teach them to think differently—God's way.

Ministerial stress frequently originates from conflict with the
congregation. In fact, I have heard some ministers express the
situation as, "Ministry would be great if you didn't have to deal
with the people." It has been said that the average church has about
two crises per week. We have to remember that we are ministering
to people, many of whom are hurting. My favorite saying is, "Hurt
people hurt people." There is a book by the same title (by Sandra
Wilson), but I did not get my saying from it. When people hurt

us, it is usually because they are in pain and want us to know it. As a result, people do not always act in a godly manner. They hurt us so that we will know they are hurting. It can also be that they are mad at God and are taking it out on us because we are God's representative. When they hurt us, it is an opportunity for us to minister to them.

In addition, church conflict unfortunately originates from church politics. As a result, an increasing number of ministers are being fired, and often over nothing other than politics. If that is not bad enough, sometimes other ministers and staff personnel can deal a lot of misery for us. Understand that these sorts of things are what we signed up for when we answered God's call to go into the ministry. God will never allow more to be put on us than we can handle.

> There hath no temptation (adversity, putting to proof) taken you but such as is common to man: but God is faithful, who will not suffer you to be tempted above that ye are able; but will with the temptation also make a way to escape, that ye may be able to bear it. (1 Cor. 10:13)

Probably one of the most beneficial tools to use in dealing with congregational issues is to teach people how God instructs us to do church. Ministers are a gift from God to the church, and they are to be followed. By the way, the term *submit* used here (1 Cor. 16:16) is analogous to our military term *fall in*. In other words, get in line and follow the leader, the minister.

And he gave some, apostles; and some, prophets; and some, evangelists; and some, pastors and teachers; For the perfecting of the saints, for the work of the ministry, for the edifying of the body of Christ. (Eph. 4:11–12)

That ye submit yourselves unto such, and to everyone that helpeth with *us*, and laboureth. (1 Cor. 16:16)

I highly recommend *Generation to Generation* by E. H. Friedman, written to help ministers better understand and deal with various congregational issues. Friedman is a psychologist and is in a leadership position in a Jewish congregation. One of his primary points is to not throw more wood on the fire, but to throw water. In other words, try to look at most situations with humor. For example, if the Sunday school teacher comes to you tells you that your son was acting badly in class this morning, you might say, "If you think that was bad, you should see him at home." Humor may not be suitable for all occasions, but hopefully you get the general idea: don't add fuel to the fire by becoming defensive. If you are handed a snake, drop it immediately.

If you are being accused of immoral or criminal activities, and you are innocent, that is a different story. You should certainly defend yourself against those accusations.

If people say or do something that upsets you, you are letting them control your emotions. Do not give up your power and let them control you. If someone hands you a snake, drop it immediately. Stay in control of your emotions. It is their problem—do not make it yours.

Marriage and family issues account for about 20 percent of ministerial stress. About 70 percent of the stress is in the organizational structure of the church, ministry, or denomination, and 10 percent is from miscellaneous matters. Most stress seems to occur at three years, again at six to twelve years, and again at twenty years, provided you stay at the same church that long.

Across denominations, about 50 percent of pastors leave the pulpit within five years. For Southern Baptist pastors, the average tenure is about eighteen months to two years. Needless to say, such short stays hurt those churches. Young and inexperienced ministers have the highest incidence of burnout. That is one main reason for writing this book—so that it doesn't happen to you. We do not want you to burnout. We want you to finish the course well.

Did Jesus and the apostles have any stress? Why do you think you will have it any easier than they did? In this world, if you are a minister, then you are a nail, and you can expect to be hammered. It is part of God's growth process for you.

It is extremely important to understand that stress is good for you, but distress is bad for you. Distress results from the improper emotional reaction to stress. Think about professional football players. They have to do weight lifting (stressful), push heavy objects around the football field (stressful), and more in order to build up and maintain their strength. In much the same way, stress in the ministry is designed to build up and maintain your strength (faith in God and His goodness). As you grow in your faith, it sets the right example for your people.

Christ said we would have stress.

> These things I have spoken unto you, that in me ye might have peace. *In the world ye shall have tribulation*: but be of good cheer; I have overcome the world. (John 16:33)

> Confirming the souls of the disciples, *and* exhorting them to continue in the faith, and *that we must through much tribulation* enter into the kingdom of God. (Acts 14:22)

H. B. London says, "Just as marital problems can derail a pastor's ministry, so can wayward children. When problems arise, *a pastor must remember that his kids are worth more than his reputation and that doing the right thing is what makes a good impression—not the other way around.*"

This is also borne out by an informal survey of Texas Baptist pastors in 2004 found that 80 percent of pastor's kids are no longer connected to the church. One current example of a pastor's child leaving the faith is that of pop star Katy Perry. She stated in an interview that she is no longer a Christian and doesn't believe in heaven, hell, or "an old man sitting on a throne" (Dale Hudson, relevantchildrensministry.com). Such actions and statements by one's child are very stressful and embarrassing, especially for a minister.

Why do you suppose this is happening? Could it be that these kids feel that the dad does not love them as he should? Maybe the kids feel that God has stolen their dad from them. What about your kids? How do they feel about you and your ministry? Does your ministry and family life draw your children closer to God, or does it push them away from God? How do you know? Have you ever asked them?

Supervision of others produces stress, as does over commitment and constant guilt feelings. Guilt feelings, as opposed to real guilt, are known as a secondary emotion. By that I mean there is another emotion under them, and usually it is resentment. A need expressed by a church member does not signify a call for you to fulfill it. How often is that phone call simply your own ego telling you that you must be important because you are "needed"? To the extent that you over function, you will be distressed. Think about it: if you do everything, you rob your people of the opportunity to serve. If you have all the answers, you weaken your people by not making them do some Bible study. For instance, if someone asks, "Where does the Bible say we cannot lose our salvation?" You might suggest they read John chapter 10, or maybe suggest they read 1 John. That way they are forced to read the Word and hopefully grow from it.

Please understand that stress is good for you and is necessary for you, whereas distress is painful and can kill you. Distress occurs when we do not respond to stress properly. Stress is essential to grow your faith.

> My brethren, count it all joy when ye fall into divers temptations; Knowing [this], that the trying of your faith worketh patience. But let patience have [her] perfect work, that ye may be perfect and entire, wanting nothing. (James 1:2–4)

> And not only *so*, but we glory in tribulations also: knowing *that tribulation worketh patience.* (Rom. 5:3)

One excellent way of dealing with stress is to follow the Serenity Prayer, which says, "God grant me the serenity to accept the things I cannot change, the courage to change the things that I can, and the wisdom to know the difference." How much time each day do you spend creating serenity in yourself and your life?

Ask God for the wisdom to tell the difference between what He wants you to change and what He wants you to accept. Then accept the things you cannot change. You will run across this statement in this book: "If someone hands you a snake, drop it." That statement conveys the idea of letting go of things you cannot change, like traffic, other people, and the economy. Let go and trust God that He knows what He is doing in your life, the church, and the world.

Another excellent way to deal with stress is to remember and use the acronym BRAIN: breathe, relax, ask, imagine, and notice. In other words, take several deep breaths and hold them for a count of four, release each breath slowly, and say out loud "Relax." Then ask yourself "How do I want to feel?" Once you decide on how you want to feel, imagine yourself in a situation feeling that way, and then notice the change in your emotions and body. Altogether, this may take five or six minutes (Bill Crawford, *Life from the Top of the Mind*).

The bottom line is that when we are in a stressful situation, God wants us to change, to be thankful, and to grow in faith. Stress always tells us that something needs to change; usually it is you, not the situation. We are to control our emotions and not let them control us. And we can do that by making certain conscious decisions like thanking God for the situation and the stress, deciding to do some deep breathing, and listening to what God says we are to learn or change as a result of the situation. Sometimes He may say, "Wait. I'll tell you later."

CHAPTER 4

BURNOUT

BURNOUT IS THE state of exhaustion and dysfunction, which causes a loss of energy, persistence, compassion, joy, and satisfaction in the work of the ministry. Some of the warning signs of burnout are a loss of focus and clarity of thinking, loss of the passion for the ministry, a tendency to feel hopeless and isolate yourself from others, loss of desire to solve problems, loss of patience, seeing ministry as work rather than God's calling on your life, and wanting to run away from new challenges. Very often a minister in burnout does not feel like working up lessons or a sermon and instead chooses to copy other minister's material.

Mismanaged stress (i.e., distress) produces burnout. Burnout is often the result of taking responsibility that is not yours, not knowing how to handle your emotions in a healthy manner, or failing to do so. You hopefully balance your checkbook regularly, but do you ever balance your emotional bank account?

How do you balance your emotional bank account? Begin by thanking God for whatever problems or stress that you are having (Eph. 5:20). Then ask Him what He wants you to learn or change. Next, listen very carefully and do what He tells you. Even if you are feeling depressed and don't know why, thank God for that emotion.

Burnout normally occurs when we take responsibility that is not ours to begin with—such as trying to change someone, motivate the people (the Holy Spirit's job), growing the ministry (numbers are God's job) rather than equipping your people to do the work of the ministry, solving all the problems (weakens your people and robs them of an opportunity to grow), or being super-Christian (nonhuman; the people cannot relate with you if you never have problems). Christ took on human form and endured all of our temptations so that we could relate to Him.

Trying to do everything yourself is similar to the children of Israel deciding to attack Ai in their own power. They wound up in defeat and a meltdown.

> And Joshua sent men from Jericho to Ai, which is beside Bethaven, on the east side of Bethel, and spake unto them, saying, Go up and view the country. And the men went up and viewed Ai. And they returned to Joshua, and said unto him, Let not all the people go up; but let about two or three thousand men go up and smite Ai; and make not all the people to labour thither; for they are but few. So there went up thither of the people about three

thousand men: and *they fled before the men of Ai.*
And the men of Ai smote of them about thirty and
six men: for they chased them from before the gate
even unto Shebarim, and smote them in the going
down: wherefore *the hearts of the people melted, and
became as water.* (Josh. 7:2–5)

How can you avoid burnout? There are a number of things to do
and not to do, and I will mention just a few.

When we encounter a lot of stress, there is often a natural
tendency to blame God for it. After all, isn't He in control? Please
do not ever blame God as Adam and Eve did, by not taking personal
responsibility for their actions when asked what they had done.

And the man said, The woman *whom thou gavest* to
be with me (Gen. 3:12)

And the woman said, The serpent [meaning "which
you created"](Gen. 3:13)

In all this Job sinned not, *nor charged God foolishly.*
(Job 1:22)

Let the situation change you, not you (or God) change the situation.
Another suggestion is that if someone hands you a snake (hurt, pain,
criticism), drop it immediately. You should consider the situation,
but do not take it personally even though it may have been meant
that way ("hurt people hurt people").

If you are the one in your family with the answer to every family problem, you are weakening your family. The same thing is true in your ministry. Likewise, the church is weakened because they become unduly dependent on you rather than upon God and stop growing.

Another way to help prevent burnout, or at least minimize its effects, and to effectively handle stress is to follow God's example and have a weekly Sabbath. If God took a weekly break, why do you think you need any less? Think about it this way: the first three commandments are about idolatry—in other words, worship and relationship with God. The fifth through tenth commandments deal with relationships with others. The fourth commandment is a hinge between a relationship with God (vertical) and a relationship (horizontal) with others. The Sabbath was the connection between the two.

A good Sabbath day (not necessarily Saturday) for you means no cell phone or computer; it's a time to be with God, yourself, your family, and God's creation. "Shabbat (Sabbath) is considered *a festive day*, when a person is *freed from the regular labors of everyday life*, can contemplate the spiritual aspects of life, and can spend time with family. Traditionally, three *festive meals* are eaten" (Wikipedia). Does this describe your Sabbath? What is the nature of your Sabbath, regardless of whenever it may be?

> And God blessed the seventh day, and sanctified it: because that in it he had rested [delight, joy (God

was *in awe of his creation and Himself*)] from all his
work which God created and made. (Gen. 2:3)

A yearly vacation is also necessary for you to maintain effectiveness.
Don't be misled by the idea that the church cannot do without you
for a week or two. That idea that you are so needed is simply an ego
trip—in other words, pride!

A lot of ministers feel as though they need to be on call twenty-
four seven. This is an ego trip because it makes you feel needed
and important. But if you do not take good care of your health and
emotions, how can you effectively minister to your people? After
all, the Bible says we are to make disciples—in other words, teach
them by our example. What does your example teach your people?
If you feel like you have to do everything, and you do it perfectly,
how does God get any glory?

Maybe you are one of those folks who think, "The devil never
takes a holiday, so why should I take one?" If you are, who do you
want to use as a role model, the devil or God?

As I stated earlier, every time you run into a difficult problem,
it is God ringing your phone. He wants to hear two things when
you answer that call. First, "Thanks for this situation," and second,
"What do you want me to change or learn?"

> Giving thanks always for all things unto God and
> the Father in the name of our Lord Jesus Christ.
> (Eph. 5:20)

The very best coping skill is to love what you are doing. Love is a decision! It is absolutely essential that you focus on the purpose and not on the pain. God wants to grow you, and He does that by allowing stress in your life.

Determine which emotions you are experiencing.

1. Take full responsibility for all of your emotions. Do not blame anyone else for them. They come from inside you and are the result of a decision you make either consciously or unconsciously.

2. Take a "trip in," and then ask yourself what a good, loving response should be.

3. Make a conscious decision to respond properly (i.e., in a godly manner).

4. Remember: *stressed* spelled backwards is *desserts*. King David said it this way in Psa. 23:6 Surely goodness and mercy shall follow me all the days of my life. The key word here is "follow." Usually we have to get through the difficult situation and then look "back" to see God's goodness and mercy there.

Some surveys say that an estimated 1,000 SBC pastors leave the ministry each year. Will you be one of those, or will you stay the course? Other denominations are experiencing a similar problem.

CHAPTER 5

CHURCH AS A FAMILY

YOU WILL FIND a few statements from this chapter repeated in the following chapter, "Why Churches Do What They Do?" This occurs because the two subjects are so closely related. This chapter's primary focus is on the actual dynamics involved, and the next chapter does not have the same focus.

The local church is a family and acts like a family; in other words, it operates with family dynamics. So what is a family? In today's culture, you will usually get different answers from different people. For instance, the 1949 *Webster's Dictionary* had five definitions of a family, but by 1989 it had fifteen definitions.

Today, that definition is an explosive and politically sensitive issue. Regardless of the definition, it is a system much like an old wind-up clock. Think of the gears with teeth that interact with other gears. If one of the gears loses or gains a tooth, one of two things normally happens: all the other gears must change, or that gear gets ejected. A third option is that it stops operating (gets stuck, shuts down).

Back in "ancient" times, when we had to manually shift gears in the car, if one of the transmission gears lost a tooth, it was not unusual for that gear to be thrown out through the transmission case. A family example of this dynamic occurs in some religions when one family member becomes a Christian, and the family kicks him or her out of the family and disowns that person.

I would like to use an analogy of a particular family to illustrate some things about the typical church family—that of Joseph and Mary. God chose Mary, probably the most unlikely, unexpected female in the world, to give birth to His son, Jesus. By the same token, God chose the most unexpected and unlikely organism to "give birth" to His children: the church.

Joseph was the stepdad to God's son; he had nothing to do with the conception of that son. It was his responsibility to care for his wife and child, to provide for their needs, to be loyal to his wife, and to teach children what he knew. He was a carpenter and taught the Son that trade, how to build things. The pastor of the majority of churches today is the stepdad (he did not start the church but had a predecessor), and the congregation are the step kids. The pastor has the same responsibilities that Joseph had.

Please allow me to express one of my biased opinions at this point. You do not have to agree with me, but please carefully consider it. I am convinced that one of the primary contributors to divorce among Christian couples today is the fact that most pastors are not being faithful to their churches. By this I mean they move from church to church (e.g., wife to wife) seeking more money, recognition, fame, or whatever. Romans 11:29, 2 Corinthians 11:2, and 1 Corinthians 4:1–2 say to me that if God calls a pastor to a specific church, he is to stay there because God does not change His mind. God can and sometimes does move you, but before you move, make sure it is God moving you and not just your fleshly desires.

> For the gifts and *calling of God are without repentance.* (Rom. 11:29)

> For I am jealous over you with godly jealousy: for I have espoused you to *one husband,* that I may present you as a chaste virgin to Christ. (2 Cor. 11:2)

You might say that the husband referred to in 2 Corinthians 11:2 is Christ, and you might be correct. But if you are, why does the husband go on to say that he wants to present them to Christ? It could also refer to one pastor as indicated in Romans 11:29. In fact, some churches have a marriage ceremony between the pastor and the church. The pastor marries that church for life.

> Let a man so account of us, as of the ministers of Christ, and stewards of the mysteries of God. Moreover it is required in stewards, *that a man be found faithful.* (1 Cor. 4:1–2)

We are to be faithful to God *and* to the church that calls us. Do you really believe that looking at other churches is being faithful?

One common issue is that the church (family) has not been taught how God says to do church. Or we might say it this way: dad (stepdad) has not taught the kids (church) how to behave, so the kids (church) are ignorant. How should we do church God's way?

A simplified approach is as follows.

a. And God hath set some in the church, first apostles, secondarily prophets, thirdly teachers, after that miracles, then gifts of healings, helps, governments, diversities of tongues. (1 Cor. 12:28)

b. And he gave some, apostles; and some, prophets; and some, evangelists; and some, pastors and teachers. (Eph. 4:11)

c. Obey them that have the rule over you, and submit yourselves: for they watch for your souls, as they that must give account, that they may do it with joy, and not with grief: for that *is* unprofitable for you. (Heb. 13:17)

d. Let the elders that rule well be counted worthy of double honour, especially they who labour in the word and doctrine. (1 Tim. 5:17)

In other words, the pastors and leaders are God's gift to the church, and they are to be followed and respected by the congregation if they are following Christ. We appear to be living in a time when congregations do not have much (if any) respect for ministers. Some think we are in the Laodician church age. Laodicia means "people (laity) rule." Many churches today are led by the people rather than the ministers.

One pastor expresses the correct way as, "Follow me or fire me." Many pastors are afraid to take such a biblical stand.

As with any "family," there will be disagreements, so don't be surprised when they occur. We all see the world through different eyes, it results in different perspectives. This provides an opportunity for a relevant discussion.

Most churches today are blended families, and they are subject to blended family dynamics. By blended families, I mean the current pastor is not the founding pastor.

The current pastor is a "stepdad," and his wife, if married, is a "stepmom." There is usually some resentment toward stepdad by the step kids in the beginning, and it takes time to overcome it. Most of the time, it takes five to seven years for a new pastor to gain the confidence, love, respect, and control (guidance) of the step kids. Statistically, about one-third of the step kids will accept you fairly quickly, about one-third of them will take longer, and about one third may never accept you. You can make the transition easier and faster if you can find the "real pastor" of the church—in other words, the person with lots of influence with the step kids. Seek his help and advice on leading the church/ministry. This is reality, and you need to be prepared for it. I believe this is one main reason so many pastors move so often: they are not aware of this kind of situation.

As a new pastor, one of the worst things you can do is to fire the existing staff and bring on new staff. The existing staff can help you be accepted by the people much faster than a new staff, which will normally alienate the people even more. Remember that the people have lost their "dad" and are usually hurting. Simply try ministering to their pain.

Certainly there are churches that never seem to accept a pastor. I know of a church near Dallas, Texas, that calls a new pastor nearly every year. Before you ever accept the call to go to a church, you should do some exploratory work. Find out how many predecessors there have been, how long each stayed, why they left, and how they left. Once you have this information, you have a much better idea of what to expect if you accept their call.

In our culture, stepmom has a very negative stereotype—that of Cinderella's stepmother. It is not the same in other cultures; for example, the very term for stepmother in French means "sweet mother." It usually takes longer for a stepmom to be accepted by the step kids than it does for a stepdad. There is often one lady in the congregation (a big sister type) who has a lot of influence. It helps a lot if stepmom seeks her advice and help in being accepted by the step kids.

What about staff positions? Where do they fit into the family? In one sense, they are like the big brother or sister—that is, if they have been there a while. A new staff member, in many cases, is seen as an adopted child or, worse, an illegitimate child. Here again it will take time to win the people over.

CHAPTER **6**

WHY CHURCHES DO
WHAT THEY DO

REMEMBER, I WILL be using the terms *minister, pastor, father, dad, stepdad,* and *stepfather,* and they all apply in general to male and female ministers. Also, I tend to use the pronoun *he* to refer to both male and female ministers.

Why do churches do what they do? First of all, we minister to "broken" people and "broken" churches. Broken people are those who have been hurt somehow and are still hurting or have issues that they have not dealt with properly. As a general rule, they are folks who have been hurt in some way by someone and have not recovered, or for some reason they do not wish to take the necessary steps to recover.

For instance, dysfunctional families have three unwritten rules: don't talk, don't feel, and don't trust. Very often there are loyalty issues, or perhaps I should say disloyalty issues, which usually stem from a lack of trust.

Because the church is a family, some churches are also dysfunctional for the very same reasons. The bottom line is that they do not know how to be in relationship or refuse to be for various reasons. Chapter seven provides more detailed information on the family dynamics involved.

One way a church can be broken is because the pastor left or the way in which he left. Another aspect of broken people and churches is that they tend to keep secrets. Secrets divide families and churches. There are those who know the secret and those who do not. When most folks all have the same information, they usually come up with the same conclusions.

There are some things in the church who do not have to be broadcast to the whole church, like staff salaries.

Some denominations and churches rotate pastors every so often. Such changes can foster a perpetual brokenness. Because of the constant changes, there is no time for the dynamics to die down. Such change, loss, shift in loyalties, and switching directions is very stressful on the congregation. There is neither a solid foundation nor a sense of security, so the development of mature disciples could be greatly hindered, if not impossible. One denomination that used to change pastors about every four years or so has realized the problems that it creates and has started changing their guidelines.

People tend to gravitate to churches that function similar to the families in which they grew up. For example, if we grew up in a very rigid family, we will tend to join a church that is very ritualistic in its worship and operation. At the other end of the spectrum, if we grew up in a chaotic family situation, we will tend to join a church that's chaotic in worship and operation, like a very charismatic one. These tendencies are usually true for both ministers and congregations.

All families have disagreements, and the church family is no exception. God wants us as ministers to grow up, and the disagreements are opportunities for both the minister and church to grow in faith and emotional maturity. We may not be able to solve every problem, but we can grow from every problem, or at least grow in our faith in God. The church is a family and is subject to family dynamics, much like any other family.

Something else to consider: one understanding of the Church of Laodicea is that it represents a majority of churches today. The term Laodicea actually means "laity led." That is what we often see, because the people have lost respect for ministers. It also is more interested in pleasing man than God. Among its characteristics listed in Revelation is that God has no good thing to say about it. It does appear to be the prominent church for the end of the "Church Age." God says ministers are a gift from Him to the church, and they are to be followed by the church.

> And unto the angel of the church of the Laodiceans
> write; These things saith the Amen, the faithful and
> true witness, the beginning of the creation of God;

I know thy works, that *thou art neither cold nor hot*:
I would thou wert cold or hot. (Rev. 3:14–15)

Young churches, like many young ministers, can focus more on doing for God rather than listening to God and then doing what He says. This behavior can cause them to stumble and fall. Most churches and ministries today are what we might call blended, step, or broken families. By that I mean the founding minister has been replaced, and the result is a family that looks like and acts like a blended (broken) family—or if you prefer, a stepfamily or remarried family. The "father" has been replaced by a "stepfather."

In a broken family, the stepchildren (congregation) tend to initially resent the stepfather. They normally feel like the stepfather is the reason the "real dad" is not there. As a general rule, children want their biological parents to be together, and a stepparent is the "enemy" who keeps this from happening. That normally results in the stepchildren resenting the stepparent. It usually takes about five to seven years for a stepparent to be accepted and gain some semblance of control of the stepchildren.

Start thinking about what this means if you as a minister move to a different ministry or church. I will be using the term *church* and *pastor,* but the same dynamics apply to ministers and ministries like the youth ministry or music ministry. You may experience a lot of rejection for a while. It is not "the devil is in this church," but the truth is that the people are hurting because they have experienced the loss of a spiritual dad. The sooner you understand and accept that the step kids are hurting, and the sooner you start ministering to their pain, the sooner they will accept you and your leadership. Once they accept you, they will begin to start loving you.

Another major factor in this dynamic is why and how they lost their "dad." If "dad" left to go to another church, that feels like a dad who leaves his wife and kids for another woman. If they have negative feelings toward the "dad," they will tend to take them out on you. They may feel that you will do just like the "dad" did and leave them too. This means they may not trust you, and hence they will hesitate to follow you. You have to remember they are hurting and then act accordingly.

Part of the dynamic at work is how the dad left the family? Did he give them any warning and time enough for the kids to accept that fact? Was there some kind of fellowship gathering at which the kids could each get a chance to say good-bye and bring some closure to that relationship?

Such a fellowship provides the opportunity for the congregation to bring closure to the relationship with the exiting pastor. When enough warning is given, and the reason for leaving is legitimate (like retirement because of age or health issues) along with an appropriate good-bye fellowship, the negative impact on the family is minimized.

Regardless of why and how the dad left, it will take time and effort for you as stepdad to gain the step kids' trust and respect. They are afraid you might leave them. They have had their hearts ripped out and are somewhat afraid that if they start to love you, it might happen again.

Before you consider leaving a church or ministry, be sure to give a lot of prayer and consideration about how your leaving is going to affect that particular body of Christ, that family. Seek counseling and do some careful investigation of what has been going on inside that church. You surely do not want to get into a bad situation. It is not unusual for the vision of a big increase in salary or a larger congregation, or even a promotion in position, to feel like God's call, but it is not. Do you really believe that God will bless you and your ministry when you hurt part of His family?

Another potential issue in broken churches is that the pastor retires and stays at that church. That situation certainly will be tough for you because the kids will still want him to do the weddings, funerals, and more. Don't let that hurt your feelings; simply be aware that these things happen, and it is not about you. They love the "dad" and not the "stepdad." If you stay there long enough, they will probably change and start loving you. If you started the church where you are, you are the spiritual father to those folks.

You can expect all types of complaints from the step kids, so don't be surprised. Remember that *the problem is never the problem.* If the problem cannot be solved rationally, it is an emotional or spiritual issue. Find out where they are emotionally and help them and their emotions. When they have a "father issue" or an issue with God, they will tend to take it out on you. You are God's representative and their spiritual father. Expect to catch a lot of garbage that is not really about you at all.

We cannot overlook spiritual problems in the church. These can occur for various reasons, such as the example set by the previous pastor, false doctrines, lack of spiritual knowledge and maturity, and satanic attacks. Satanic attacks can come from within the church body or from the outside, like the city, the neighborhood, and more. Here again, every problem is an opportunity for spiritual and emotional growth. You can expect to have some conflicts with other ministers in the church. Even the disciples had conflicts with each other at times. My studies and personal experience demonstrate that when one answers God's call to go into the ministry, that person signs up for a multitude of problems. That includes problems even from within one's own family.

Another area of concern is that of finances and giving. In 2 Corinthians 9:7, it says, "Every man according as he purposeth in his heart, so let him give; not grudgingly, *or of necessity*: for God loveth a cheerful giver." If the church is has a financial need, teach the people to give to God out of thankfulness for all of His goodness to them, not out of necessity.

Another way of thinking about this is to pray down funds rather than raising them. Try not to borrow money, because God has enough to pay cash for whatever He wants. He will supply the needed funds on His schedule and not necessarily on your schedule, provided the need is what He desires. When you borrow money, you become a slave to the lender. There two kinds of people, givers and takers. Which kind are you?

An interesting survey by Mobilecause.com says that different generations have a tendency to give differently. Of the millennials (1980–1995) 60 percent tend to give to causes, not organizations. For Generation X (1965–1979), 59 percent give to charities. For baby boomers (1945–1964), 72 percent give recurrently to charity. In the "greatest generation" (born prior to 1944), 88 percent give to charity. As a general rule the older generations tend to give more than the younger ones. This may indicate that we have not been teaching the youth in our churches the blessings of giving.

Please understand that I am prejudiced about this next point. I base it largely on Romans 11:29, "For the gifts and *calling of God* are *without repentance.*" In other words, God does not change His mind. I am talking about pastors and ministers, not evangelists, church planters, and others who, by their very calling, must move around. It is my understanding that once we are called into ministry, we are expected to minister as long as we are physically able to do so. That does not mean we may not have to have a secular job at times to adequately provide for our families. Sometimes we have to work two jobs, the ministry and a secular job.

If you are called by God to a particular church or ministry, then you are to stay there—period. God can move you if He wants to, but you had better be sure it is God and not just your desires. This is another area where you must critically evaluate your thinking and emotions. A multitude of counselors including your spouse and children is needed. (Prov.11:14)

If you look at what we normally think of as great churches or ministries, the pastors have been there a lot of years. That alone should be incentive enough for you to stay where you are. I know from personal experience what a blessing it is to marry a young couple and then a few years later baptize their children—and even marry the children. There is no substitute for long-term relationships.

In addition, when you move around from place to place, there is often a negative effect upon your children, if you have any. They often become what are known as third culture kids (TCKs).

Here are some characteristics of TCKs and the issues with which they have to deal.

1. Rootlessness—Where do I belong? Where am I from? Where is home? Who am I as a person?

2. Restlessness—Difficulty settling down, an unrealistic attachment to the past, trouble keeping a job; some feel a need to be far from parents, but some do just the opposite.

3. Relationships—Usually they have many that cannot be maintained, and they often see those in the home culture as shallow or boring. Some may jump quickly into deep relationships while others have shallow relationships keeping everyone at a distance. It's not unusual for these kids to develop marital problems.

4. Maturity—They often appear to be mature because of knowledge and experience, but they're emotionally immature, and adolescence (including rebellion) can be delayed until their late twenties or early thirties.

5. Unresolved grief—This is due to having lost friends, homes, schools, and familiar surroundings.

Some foundational building blocks for raising healthy TCK's are:

1. Having commitment to and for each other in the family

2. Respect and support for each other

3. A willingness to nurture and build each relationship

    a. Listen carefully (words) and empathetically (emotions) to each child's concerns

    b. How well do you know your children? What makes them angry? What is their love language? Do they feel loved by you as opposed to "knowing" they are loved by you?

c. Make each child feel special: spend one-on-one time with each one every day

d. Protect the children in every way

e. Do not leave them with a caregiver for extended periods so that they feel abandoned.

f. Do the children see your work as significant, or does it put a wedge between you and them?

g. Do you practice what you preach in your home?

Remember that your primary responsibility and mission field is your family. By *family*, I mean your family of origin (the one you were born into), and if you're married, your nuclear family. The ministry family comes second.

CHAPTER 7

PROBLEMS IN THE CHURCH

IN EARLIER CHAPTERS, I mentioned some problems one encounters in the church and suggested some ways to handle them. You may find a small amount of repetition in this chapter.

Life, and especially the Christian life, is all about learning how to deal with losses. Congregations have a lot of expectations and demands that they put on a minister. If you do not set up boundaries, you will spend a lot of time and effort outside your areas of gifting. This can result in frustration and anger on your part, as well as an increase in church problems. It is of the utmost importance that you minister to your family first and foremost. There is much more to life than church ministry.

> For if a man know not how to rule his own house, how
> shall he take care of the church of God? (1 Tim. 3:5)

One should ask, "Who taught this ministry to have these demands and expectations?" Was it you by your behavior, or was it your predecessor or some very influential family in the church? It appears that the average pastor spends only one-fourth of his time in direct people ministry, and yet that is the very essence of what ministry is supposed to be about. I know of one local church where the pastor even printed the weekly bulletins—and this was in a church with a secretary. His role model was apparently Martha rather than Mary.

Whenever you encounter a problem, the first thing you should do is thank God for it. That is God ringing your phone, and He wants to hear two things from you when you answer it: "Thanks for the problem," and "What do you want me to learn from it?" "Every trial is a doorway to deeper intimacy with God" (Gary Smalley).

> Giving thanks always for all things unto God and
> the Father in the name of our Lord Jesus Christ.
> (Eph. 5:20)

All families have disagreements, and the church family is no different. If an issue cannot be resolved rationally, it is emotional or spiritual. It is a disguised opportunity for you to minister to the ones bringing the issue up. Very often the real problem is in their very own family, but it is expressed in the church family.

Of course, the problem could be caused by the pastor. Often this type problem is caused by a wrong focus of the pastor or staff. Quality is the keyword, because we are playing for keeps, for eternity. Quality equals love.

Are you ministering to meet your own needs or those of your people? Which glorifies God more? Some ministers work harder on their people's spiritual well-being than the people are working. When we do that, we are over functioning as parents and are being ineffective as shepherds. We have let the people give us their jobs. Here is one of the areas where boundaries are so important. John Maxwell stated it this way: "I am responsible to you but not for you." You cannot control the decisions that the people make.

A church becomes dysfunctional for the same reasons that any family does. That means the kids (congregation) normally reflect the dad's (pastor's) attitudes. What you do in moderation, your kids will tend to do in excess.

One example is if the pastor had his personal agenda as a higher priority than his personal family. One pastor in particular set as his personal goal, while in seminary, to pastor a very large church in Dallas. He managed to move from church to church and finally reached his goal, but then he wound up divorced and at last report was selling cemetery plots.

Be sure you are sensitive to God's call and not your own ambition and desires. It is easy to fall into the trap of desiring a larger church, more of a spotlight, increased income, etc. and mistake the emotion/ desire for the voice of the Holy Spirit. To avoid the trap requires a critical evaluation of one's thinking and emotions as well as seeking God's definite guidance. If you are married you should also ask your spouse their opinion. In addition, ask your children, if you have any. God says there is wisdom in the multitude of counselors. (Prov.11:14)

Another reason is the church refuses to adapt or adjust to new paradigms. One example is if the neighborhood around the church shifts ethnically, and the church ignores the change; the church normally dies or wants to change its location, in which case it misses the opportunity to minister to its neighbors.

When a minister ignores the emotions of the people, the church family can become dysfunctional. Psychology says a dysfunctional family normally has three main rules: don't feel, don't trust, and don't talk. This applies also to the church family.

The ideas of independence, individual rights, and egalitarian relationships are great in politics but *don't belong in families.* Each of you is a member of three families: family of origin (the family you were born into), family by marriage (if you are married), and the church family. Issues in any one of these families will produce symptoms in the other; failure to see and understand this often creates and aggravates problems.

The ministry is a family, and you are the "dad." The family process takes place in the church. The problem is almost never in the mind (logical); it is almost always in the emotions. That's why splits are almost never over doctrine, but over hurt feelings. If you cannot solve a problem through rational process, the issue is emotional. (Jam.4:1)

Sometimes you will hear complaints about the church not growing, and the folks blame you. It is *not* your job to grow the church numerically. Be sure to remind them that it is God's job to grow the church numerically, and that they should be doing the work of the ministry (witnessing, etc.).

Words are not as important as the emotions and the motivation underlying them. "You are a terrible preacher." What are possible issues beneath the surface of this statement? There may be some truth in it, but more likely it is an issue with God or a parent. It is also possible people simply want some of your attention. It does show that they are in pain, and this is a good opportunity for you to explore what and why they are feeling and minister to them. Never take criticism personally. If there is truth in it, remedy the problem. If the criticism is not valid, drop it like a snake and don't let it bite you.

For example, a mother knitted two sweaters and sent them to her son. Sometime later, she was coming to visit him. In order to please her, he wore one of the sweaters when he met her at the airport. She saw the sweater and said, "So what's the matter? Didn't you like the other one?" Most criticism will not go away by trying harder to please.

Here are some helpful guidelines to help you avoid problems and to help deal with them when they arise.

1. Teach your people to love and trust God and each other; we only teach by example.

2. A church without dreamers is a dead one. Are you a dreamer? Why not?

3. Explore with new members what attracted them to your ministry.

4. Never talk about any church member to another church member.

5. Review the giving record of all candidates for church offices before election or nomination. Do the same before seeing people coming in to see you. This may sound weird to you, but consider it. If people are not giving to God and the church, their hearts are not in the church, and therefore they do not have a word from God for you or the best interests of the church at heart. A change in the giving record of a person or family often indicates a "sick sheep" that needs the shepherd's attention. This is not about giving per se, but how the family is doing overall.

6. If you (really, the Holy Spirit) can't build a church where you are, you can't build one anywhere. Besides that, it is not your job to build the church. That is God's job ("upon this rock I will build my church").

7. A good staff person will pay for herself in a year's time. She really does not cost the church anything. You always get what you pay for.

8. God is able to pay cash for anything He wants done.

9. It's not about how many people you have in your church—it's how many ministers you have in the pew. That is the Great Commission!

10. God will not bless your plan if you have a backup plan.

11. If you are the pastor, you cannot effectively counsel members of your church, other than spiritually. The main reason is that if a member comes to you with a problem. and God is leading you to bring a message on that subject, that member is going to feel like counseling with you is not confidential because you are preaching about his or her situation. One solution is to arrange with the pastor of a different church to counsel with each other's members.

12. Your family is your primary ministry and God's work more than anything else, including the church.

13. If you counsel with people of the opposite sex, do not mention your emotions to them. They can tell you all of their emotions, but if you tell them some of yours, you run the risk of becoming emotionally involved with them.

Crossing this emotional line is what has resulted in many ministers falling into sexual sin. To protect yourself, never cross this emotional line.

Congregational Issues

A problem with a church member is usually an unresolved problem with that person's family in disguise. Recognizing this diminishes the intensity of the attack, takes pressure off of you, and keeps you from being the symptom bearer for the whole church.

Remember that the problem is never the problem, but it usually is a metaphor for the real problem. There are many illustrations of this: complaints about your unavailability often have to do with issues of abandonment; the person who never says no when asked to perform some service around the church is often looking for acceptance and approval; the person who has been abused somehow and, when questioned about it, shrugs it off usually feels like she must have caused or deserved the abuse. Adults who had traumatic childhoods can result in them having major depression (Dr. David Stoop). And then there is the person who always asks, "Why do you always have to have things your way?" Here is a person who probably feels like her opinion never matters.

People in a church tend to gravitate toward the same family roles they had in their families of origin, and they tend to seek churches that relate as their families did. In other words, if they grew up in a chaotic family, they will seek a church whose worship style is somewhat chaotic; if they come from a very rigid family, they will seek a legalistic or ritualistic church.

If the issue cannot be resolved rationally, it is an emotional issue. When your children bicker among themselves at home, that might indicate they want their parents' attention. It's true in church too, so give them some attention. Conflicts are part of family relationships and are not to be feared or considered as signs of poor emotional or spiritual health. Hurt people hurt people!

Criticism and Complaints

You will get most complaints when you are doing your most efficient and effective job. Part of this response is due to the fact that changes are taking place, and people usually do not like changes. Criticism is the adult way of crying or controlling (as with the Jewish mother and the sweaters). Criticism will often die of its own accord if not fueled by your anxiety and defensiveness. Be very careful how you respond to it.

The only way you can avoid criticism is by becoming a nonperson. "To escape criticism, do nothing, say nothing, be nothing." If you think yourself above criticism, you are not worth it.

> Whoso loveth instruction loveth knowledge: but
> he that hateth reproof is brutish. Brutish in the

Hebrew means (concretely) stupid: — brutish (person), foolish. (Prov. 12:1)

A fool's wrath is presently known: but a prudent man covereth shame. (Prov. 12:16)

There is that speaketh like the piercings of a sword: but the tongue of the wise is health. (Prov. 12:18)

A soft answer turneth away wrath: but grievous words stir up anger. (Prov. 15:1)

A wrathful man stirreth up strife: but he that is slow to anger appeaseth strife. (Prov. 15:18)

The foolish and the wise respond differently to criticism. Before you respond to criticism, ask yourself:

a) What is this person really saying?

b) What are the emotions involved here—theirs and mine?

c) Why do I want to say what I want to say?

d) Can I say it in love?

e) Will my response just add fuel to the fire?

Most complaining has an irrational base. Complaining is the adult way of crying to get one's way. Don't take it personally. A construction worker complained to his buddy. He would say, "Every day I have peanut butter and jelly for lunch."

His buddy asked, "Why don't you ask your wife to make you something else?"

The worker's reply was, "Oh, I make my own lunch."

"Your life is in the hands of any person who upsets you." Of course, they do not make you upset—that is a choice you make.

Certainly there are times when criticism is valid. In these cases, it is important for you to do a careful and honest self-evaluation. Ask yourself these questions, and give yourself honest answers.

1. Did you cause the conflict/problem? If you did, how can you fix it?

2. Are you prolonging it? If the answer is yes, then what do you need to do to correct things? If the answer is no, what do you need to do?

3. What would God have you learn or change as a result of this situation?

4. Have you thanked God for this situation and those involved in it? As Ephesians 5:20 and 1 Corinthians 12:18 say, He placed them in the body. It is all for your good and growth.

Some Practical Tips

1. Check the giving records of all complainers *before* they come in complaining. If they are not giving, they do not have a word from God for you because their hearts are not in your church.

2. Not everyone's tithe and gifts go for the same thing

3. Monitoring the giving records of your people can help you spot who may be having problems early on, and you may be able to minister to them. If you do this, do not talk to them about their giving, but whether or not they are having some kind of difficulty (family, business, health, etc.).

4. Check giving records of those being considered for any church office, such as teachers and deacons. Again, this helps to know whether they have their hearts in the church and are being good disciples, at least in this area.

5. Teach your people to trust God and each other. You only teach by example.

6. Teach your people to love God and each other. You have to set the example.

CHAPTER 8

PARADIGMS

AS A MINISTER, it is best if you have some idea of what to expect in the way of bumps in the road, especially if you want to have an effective ministry. This is especially true if you are somewhat new to ministry. That is one reason for this chapter: to prepare you for what lies ahead. It is also practical for those who have been in ministry a while.

A paradigm is essentially a way of thinking, a type of map or plan of the way you look at life and what is going on around you, a "how to deal with it" plan. *Merriam Webster's Dictionary* defines paradigm as "a theory or a group of ideas about how something should be done, made, or thought about." It is a lens through which you view the world around you. Much of what I have to say about paradigms was influenced by Joel Arthur Barker in his video "The Business of Discovering the Future." This is an excellent video to gain more information on paradigms.

The world around us is always changing. It is important that you make sure you are aware of the changes, because you may need to change your paradigms (the way that you think things should be done). I consider this to be especially important for ministers if they want to have effective ministries. That means sometimes you have to change the way you do things and see things.

One example is that of the ancient Hebrew religion and worship. Things went along unchanged for many centuries, and then all of a sudden Jesus Christ appeared on the scene and changed everything. As you read the account in the Bible of how the Jewish religious hierarchy responded, you see an excellent example of how religious leaders can be caught off guard by reality shifts. The religious leaders of that day refused to change their paradigms and saw that Jesus was bringing about changes that they did not want to accept. Rather than make changes, they decided to get rid of the troublemaker so that they could continue doing things the same way they had always done them. Isn't that how insanity is defined—being out of touch with reality?

A word of caution: How does an "unchanging" church deal with an ever-changing world? I am told from various sources that 85 percent of churches in America are dying. Some say that about 3 churches shut down every day. Why? By dying, I mean diminished attendance, with some vanishing as an entity. Studies show that some two hundred churches each month are closing their doors. That can be due to not taking into account how reality is changing.

Very often they refuse to see or accept changes in the world around them. For example, a congregation in a white neighborhood refuses to notice the neighborhood around them is changing ethnicity. They refuse to be a proper witness, and soon the church no longer exists. This is an example of the old saying, "Doing things the way we have always done them over and over again but expecting different results."

Another reason is that all too often, a church will change to match the culture rather than the church changing the culture. When people go to a church, they should be presented with the need and opportunity to accept Jesus as their personal Lord and savior, but a lot of churches do not give them that opportunity. I do not necessarily mean an altar call, but rather being presented with the gospel in a manner that they can understand the need and be challenged to accept Christ. Too many churches have no one saved each year. Should the church be relevant to the culture or to Christ? God never told us to fill our church building with people, but He did say that if Christ be lifted up, He would draw all men to Him. "We need to keep the main thing, the main thing" (Dr. John D. Morgan).

One reality shift that affects our ministries directly is that there is very little denominational loyalty. This can be caused by various factors, such as a change in a denomination's teachings or a stand on certain issues.

> The trend toward consumer-driven religion has
> been gaining momentum for half a century or more.

Consider that in 1955 only 15 percent of Americans said that they no longer adhered to the faith of their childhood, according to a Gallup poll. By 2008, 44 percent had switched their religious affiliation at least once, or dropped it altogether, according to the Pew Forum on Religion & Public Life. Americans now sample, dabble and move on when a religious leader fails to satisfy them for any reason. In this transformation, many clergy have seen their job descriptions rewritten by the church. In other words, what is expected of the minister is changing in many churches, They are no longer expected to offer moral counsel in pastoral care sessions or to deliver sermons that make the comfortable uneasy. Church leaders who continue such Biblical ministerial traditions pay dearly. Ministry is a profession in which the greatest rewards include meaningfulness and integrity. When these fade under pressure from churchgoers who don't want to be challenged or edified, pastors become candidates for stress and depression. (Rev. Jeffrey McDonald)

In the 2013 Annual Church Profile, 60 percent of the more than 46,000 churches in the Southern Baptist Convention (SBC) reported no youth baptisms (ages 12–17) in 2012, and 80 percent reported only one or zero baptisms among young adults (ages 18–29). One in four Southern Baptist churches reported zero baptisms overall in 2012, whereas the "only consistently growing" baptism group was children under five years old. The number of SBC churches increased, but reported membership of those churches declined by 136,764, down 0.9 percent to 15.7 million members. Primary worship attendance declined 2.21 percent to an average of 5.8 million Sunday worshippers. That means that only about one-third of church members attend worship services.

We ministers may have to change our methods, but not our message, when reality changes. Change is an unavoidable fact of life and is often not pleasant. Change is a lot like a birth, somewhat messy, whereas no change is somewhat like death, simple and done. Have you really thought about the command to go into the highways and the hedges (Luke 14:23), and what that means to you? *Hedges* in Greek is *phragmos*, which means "a fence, or enclosing barrier (literally or figuratively): — hedge (+round about), partition, a fence that which separates, prevents two from coming together."

> And the lord said unto the servant, Go out into the highways and hedges, and compel them to come in, that my house may be filled. (Luke 14:23)

Where are the hedges? Places that are off the beaten path, difficult to get through and we have to cut new trails. In fact, you may have to become a trailblazer or pioneer.

What are the hedges? Among other things, they are the uncomfortable areas, maybe even painful, and you may not be able to see where you are going. There might be poisonous snakes, biting insects, or thorny cacti. They are difficult to get through. Some of them have been designed like a fence, to hinder you from getting through them. The following paragraphs outline some of the hedges (paradigms) you will encounter in our current culture. As a minister, you need to know where the people are and what their needs are so that you can best minister to them. Some examples of fairly recent societal changes, which will probably require you to shift your paradigms (your ways of thinking about ministry), are as follows.

Focus on the Family has reported that only about 9 percent of born-again believers have a biblical worldview (Del Tackett). That being the case, you may have to do some real trail blazing in order to be able to disciple (Matt. 28:19) most born-again believers. There are no shortcuts, and that is why they are described as hedges. But I have not given up, and neither should you. King David tells us that "surely goodness and mercy shall follow me all the days of my life" (Ps. 23:6). The key word here is *follow*. You normally cannot see or feel God's goodness and mercy when you are in the midst of difficult times. That is when you have to exercise a lot of faith. You have to get through the hard times and then look back to see God's mercy and goodness in that trial. This is a tough hedge to hack through, but with the Holy Spirit's help, you can do it.

Past successes may not mean anything today. Because the world around us changes, what worked well in the past may not work at all today. A couple of examples are tent revivals and bus ministries. They were effective in their day but do not work well today. Some other examples are in the area of media. Twitter has taken over Facebook, reducing communication down to about forty words or less. The overall effect of media on our culture means what used to be high definition sound has changed with the introduction of digital electronics. There is some indication that the hearing of the younger generation has actually changed due to the digital era. The digital sound is more sterile and not as smooth, warm, and broad as analog music.

A lot of us start out as individuals and wind up as copies. We often copy other ministers rather than copying Christ. There seems to be a tendency for us in ministry to watch other ministries; if they seem to be growing in numbers, then we want to jump on their bandwagon and copy them. You must be very careful about doing this. Don't be a copier; be sure you are following God's leadership for you and your ministry. What appears to work for others may not work for you and your ministry. God blesses different ministries differently. Do not focus on numbers but on effectiveness. God measures effectiveness and success by whether or not you follow His leadership and obey Him. No one listened to Jeremiah as he preached for some thirty years, yet he was "effective" because he did exactly what God wanted him to do. In other words, are you and your ministry bringing glory to God or to yourself? When you are in the pulpit, at the podium, or on the stage, is the spotlight on you or on Christ?

What paradigms do you have that might hinder you and your ministry from being more effective? Paradigms are not bad in and of themselves; they simply are, and we should be aware of what ours are and when a reality shift (world changes) occurs. When the world around us changes, then we often have to change our paradigms (the way we view and deal with those changes) in order to be more effective.

Many of our paradigms were developed as we were growing up; in fact, most were in place by the age of ten. The part of the brain that allows us to begin to think abstractly doesn't really begin to develop until about age twelve.

Ephesians 6:12 says, "For we wrestle not against flesh and blood, but against principalities." Think about this statement for a few moments. The word *principalities* in Greek is *arche*, which is where we get the word *archeology*. It simply means beginning and is translated as such in John 1:1. What this phrase says is that the "number one" thing we wrestle with are "our beginnings"—what we inherited, what we experienced, and what we were taught growing up. In other words, it's the paradigms we were given by our parents and those we developed as young kids, such as "life should be fair." It is not the only thing we have to wrestle with, but it is number one. The Bible also refers to the "vain conversation" (1 Pet. 1:18) received from our fathers. What Peter is saying is that we inherit a lot of stuff that is a waste, which agrees with Ephesians 6:12 and the "beginning" statement. The Old Testament conveys the same idea.

> Keeping mercy for thousands, forgiving iniquity and transgression and sin, and that will by no means clear the guilty; visiting the iniquity of the fathers upon the children, and upon the

children's children, unto the third and to the fourth generation. (Exod. 34:7)

One example that illustrates the things we can inherit is given by David Stoop. "Paternal grandfather must watch his diet to insure healthy grandsons. A smoking grandfather will tend to produce overweight grandsons. Parents are like the shuttles on a loom—they join the threads of the past to those of the future leaving their patterns on the cloth." I don't know whether Dr. Stoop is a believer, but he sure agrees with the Bible on this point about what we can inherit. Another example from my own counseling experience is a family where, for three generations, the oldest daughter had a child out of wedlock.

Some of these ideas on reality were partly suggested and reinforced by The Truth Project by Focus on the Family. Reality is simply the "truth." Truth and reality are things as they are and how they relate to all things past, present, and future. Certainly the Bible also says Christ was the "truth" (John 14:6), and what is more real than Christ?

One big hedge that can be expected to become even larger is anyone who opposes a popular thought or policy. In other words you "have to be politically correct." Otherwise, you are considered racist, homophobe, uneducated, or even a terrorist. When a people turn their backs on God, they cannot think straight (Rom. 1:21–22) and become "fools." Sound thinking has to be based on a firm moral foundation, and that only comes from God.

Another tough hedge area is that 47 percent of Christians admit that pornography is a major problem in the home (Jerry Ropelato). Does this say that ministers are not preaching or teaching enough on what God has to say about sex and this sort of thing? Are you afraid to preach on sex? How often do you do it? Many, if not most, ministers seem afraid or embarrassed to speak much on this subject. This could also be contributed to by the lack of a biblical worldview by most born-again believers. The movies and television seem to be encouraging more pornography and sex in general.

> "A large amount of sexual addiction is now considered normal. This includes multiple affairs, pornography and compulsive masturbation." (John Bradshaw)

Part of that tough hedge area is that 34 percent of churchgoing women have admitted to intentionally visiting porn Web sites (*The Charlotte Observer*, 2009). How should you address this in your ministry? Would you address it? Maybe that is why it is a problem. What are you going to do about it?

Maybe the major contributor to the problem of pornography is that 43 percent of pastors have intentionally visited porn sites, according to the National Coalition of Pastors Survey (Crosswalk, 2009). Are you part of this group? If you are not, how do you protect yourself from becoming part of it? Are you going to be part of the problem or part of the solution?

Pastors know better, so why are they viewing pornography, and what can be done to help them? Very often viewing pornography is the result of emotional exhaustion on the pastors' part. Sometimes it is because they are not feeling loved, especially by mom or dad. Sometimes they do not know how to communicate their needs to others, or they're afraid to do so. Often they are afraid to discuss sexual issues in their family or the church family.

Do you know how to avoid or deal with emotional exhaustion? Sometimes it can be the result of not having felt loved by one's mother while growing up; not feeling loved by spouse, family, or church; and feeling exhausted on a Sunday night. Do you know how to handle your emotions in a healthy manner? I will give you some helpful information on how to handle your emotions later in this book.

Another related reality change needs our special attention as ministers. In the inner US cities, 66 percent of births are out of wedlock, and 33 percent of children born in California in 1995 were born into homes without a father. Has this increased or decreased? In the United States in 1960, unwed births were 5.3 percent. In 2000 it increased to 33.5 percent. By 2009 it had increased to 40 percent of births to unwed mothers. (Centers for Disease Control, National Center for Health Statistics, Division of Vital Statistics). This again shows how great a need there is to have more messages about sex and marriage. Are you doing that?

Associated with births out of wedlock is the change in age of puberty for girls. Before 1900 it was around age fourteen or fifteen, but by 1980 it had dropped to age thirteen, and currently it's around age eleven. Some fifty years ago, kids knew they were part of the community. Today, they perform and conform in order to be accepted (Chap Clark, Fuller Theological Seminary).

"Parents now spend 40% less time with their kids" (Lester C. Thurow). One in four women between the ages of fourteen and nineteen is infected with at least one of the most common sexually transmitted diseases (CDSC, March 10, 2008).

There are some eight hundred Hindu temples in the United States. Here is a real "foreign mission field" in your own neighborhood. Have you thought about how you can best witness or minister to them? Does your ministry have a missionary outreach, or do you simply focus on those folks who come in the front door of your church? The great commission tells us to teach all nations, and in some places all nations come to your town. One example is Houston, Texas, which has over ninety different languages spoken there.

The modern world is now giving way to what many writers call the postmodern world. This transformation has changed how many people view the world, how they understand reality and truth, and how they approach the fundamental questions of life. So what is it like? I'm glad you asked that question, and I will give you some idea about what it is like in the following paragraphs. Here again, you may need to change some of your paradigms in order to have a more effective ministry.

One major aspect of the postmodern world is materialism (or consumerism). We are seeing a new "religion" gaining ground every day. It is not really new, but it is rapidly coming to the forefront in our country. It is the religion of greed, with money being their god, otherwise known as loving oneself to the exclusion of others. One big example is Bernie Madoff. He demonstrated how far one can go in making money without concern about how it affects other people. Their gospel appears to be something like, "So what if people lose all their savings? So what if bankruptcies occur? So what if thousands are defrauded and hurt? If I come out ahead, all is well." (David Jeremiah, *The Coming Economic Armageddon*). The people need to be taught that they should trust God, not the dollar. It all belongs to Him anyhow.

Another aspect of the postmodern world is the placeless society. This term means we often do not have to be in a certain physical place in order to accomplish a task. One example is that we do not have to go the bank (a certain place) to make a deposit; we can do it with our cell phones. Another example is we don't have to go to church anymore because we can watch it on TV or online. For a lot of jobs, we can work from home; one large movie production company is run from the three executives' homes. How might this be affecting your ministry, and what should you do about it? Hebrews

10:25 tells us to forsake not the gathering of ourselves together. Have you preached on this command?

I am not against having church services on television and the Internet. They are great for those who are unable to attend services otherwise, plus we often can reach unchurched folks. But what about those folks who are able to attend but find it easier to simply watch services on television rather than get ready and go to church? If they are watching on TV or the Internet, you can still reach them and teach them about coming together in a church by your messages.

Kids currently do not have to go to authorities for knowledge; they can go to the Internet. When today's kids are grown, how will they feel and react toward authority figures as a result of not having to look to an authority for knowledge? Not all information on the internet is correct or true so they may be getting a lot of misinformation. For instance, will they accept the Bible as God's word, or will they listen to and follow the pastor's leadership? What should you be doing now to point the kids in the right direction? "Parents who are involved with their children tend to live longer than the uninvolved" (Dr. David Stoop).

The growth in the number and proportion of older adults is unprecedented in the history of the United States. Two factors (longer life spans and aging baby boomers) will combine to double the population of Americans aged sixty-five years or older during the next twenty-five years, to about seventy-two million. By 2030, older adults will account for roughly 20 percent of the US population. During the past century, a major shift occurred in the leading causes of death for all age groups, from infectious diseases and acute illnesses to chronic diseases and degenerative illnesses. More than one-quarter of all Americans and two-thirds of older Americans have multiple chronic conditions, and treatment for this population accounts for 66 percent of the country's health care budget (Centers for Disease Control, The State of Aging and Health in America 2013).

Everything has to be to the extreme. Extreme sports is one example. Another rather obvious one is that women tend to be showing more and more skin. Look at some of the reality television shows like *Fear Factor, Hardcore Pawn,* and many others. Notice how many major movies now appear to be science fiction or horror stories rather than telling about real life or comedies. One example is a major movie of 2014 that uses very inappropriate language several hundred times in it, so some say. Notice the ratio of "R" rated movies vs PG-13 that are being produced.

Even the animated movies for kids are "far out." A lot of restaurants try to see how much they can put on a hamburger bun. What about the size of television screens nowadays? They are almost life-sized! The only thing that is not extreme is our witnessing for Christ. How can we be more "extreme" in our witnessing for Christ in today's world? How can we better reach a generation saturated with extremes?

Another extreme we encounter is not desiring to exert much effort or work in various activities. We live in what can be called an effortless culture, which means we expect everything to be more or less automatic. We do not want to exert much, if any, effort. What effect does this have on church attendance and personal discipline? How does this atmosphere affect you, and how you do minister to it? Do you tend to make your ministry effortless? In other words, have you slacked off from what God called you to do?

Shifting from the physical to some of the mental changes in our culture. The effects of technology on your brain, according to the experts, are largely negative, especially for children (Richard Restak, *The Young Brain*). One example is the way some TV newscasts run ribbons across the bottom and often both sides of the screen while some commentator is reporting the news. Our brain is most effective when focused on a single task at a time.

There are many other examples, such as texting while driving. Others include social media and its effect on communication, many of the video games, and the mixing of text and graphics at the same time. Too much information is given, and it tends to scramble the brain. Some researchers claim such things are the cause of, or at least contribute to, attention deficit disorder (ADD) in children. Add to these apparent changes in attention span and ability to focus. The brain is designed to perform one primary task at a time. We talk about multitasking, but actually our brain cannot multitask very well at all.

Are you aware that most schools are no longer teaching handwriting (cursive)? Schools have also gotten away from teaching the students to think critically. As I mean it here, critical thinking is the careful and detailed evaluation of an idea and research of its validity. Critical thinking is very important, and yet it appears that our educational system is not teaching students how to do it, or even discussing the need for it. Yet the basis of success in almost every area of life is thinking. Many educational leaders say the educational system is dumbing down our students. In fact, one of several books discussing this is entitled *The Dumbing Down of America* by Val "Rocky" Patterson. There are several other books on the subject.

Why are these educational issues of concern to you as a minister? For one thing, it affects the way in which you can effectively communicate with the younger generations. For example, if their attention span is shorter, a longer sermons and lessons are lost on them. They interact but do not really communicate. You have to get the message across quickly before you lose their attention. It can help to have something like PowerPoint along with the message. Additionally, how are these things going to affect the next generation of ministers?

"Indeed, if our survey measurements are correct, each new generation is literally reinventing God in an image that points toward an acceptance and appreciation of our pluralistic world." This is what neuroscientists at the University of Pennsylvania have said (Andrew Newberg and Mark Robert Waldman, *"How God*

Changes the Brain). How can you, in your ministry, help correct this changing view of God? Do you have a biblical view of God? We normally put our dad's face on God and wind up feeling toward God the way we feel toward Dad. Any negative feelings that you have toward anyone are directed toward God (Luke 10:16; 1 Thess. 4:8). The key word in these passages is *atheteō*, translated as *despiseth*. It represents almost any negative emotion. Make sure you do not have any negative feelings toward your dad. God gave you exactly the dad you needed to become the person He wants you to be.

> He that heareth you heareth me; and he that despiseth you despiseth me; and he that despiseth me despiseth him that sent me. (Luke 10:16)

> He therefore that despiseth, despiseth not man, but God, who hath also given unto us his holy Spirit. (1 Thess. 4:8)

The new paradigm of the "typical family" is of particular importance to us in ministry, because the family is the very foundation of every society, and especially of a church and even a nation. Is your paradigm of the typical American family one where it is a first marriage, the husband is the breadwinner, the wife is a homemaker, and the children are theirs? If that is your paradigm, what percentage of American families does that represent? Fairly recent surveys show it to be less than 10 percent. How should this change affect your ministry to families? Notice some of the past change: 30 percent are single parent, 55 percent of households are married couples married couples with children under eighteen was 50 percent in 1970, and

18 percent in 1997, married adults was 75 percent in 1972 and 56 percent in 1997, married couples with children was 45 percent in the 1970s and 26 percent by 1998. Now, unmarried adults make up nearly 50 percent of American households—and then we also have homosexual marriages.

It is not just in America that we see reality has changed. For instance, in "Russia during the first quarter of 2002 the divorce rate increased 38.2% and the number of divorces exceeded the number of marriages. In Japan the divorce rate has doubled over the past 16 years while in China divorce rate has increased 700% over past 15 years" (*Today's Family International Update*, 1/10/2003). These changes should affect the approach a missionary uses to minister to these folks. In America, where the divorce rate is about 50 percent even among Christians, there is a new idea starting to be used. Rather than calling it divorce, they are suggesting it be called uncoupling. I guess that is supposed to take the pain out of divorce. Are you preaching any messages that teach the sanctity of marriage, what it represents, and what God has to say about divorce?

Women generally feel the need to be in a "happy" marriage, whereas men are satisfied to simply be married. This may help explain why women initiate 75 percent of divorces (Beth M. Erickson, *Longing for Dad*).

God hates divorce but not the people involved. Think about Jesus and the Samaritan woman (John 4). She had been married five times. It is doubtful that all of her husbands had died; most likely she had been divorced one or more times. Jesus did not condemn her for that or for living with some guy without being married to him.

Certainly we live in the digital era. One example is how many folks are on their cell phones everywhere, even when driving.

> Americans average 115 texts on their phones each day. In terms of television and the internet we find that since 2000 the number of "reality" shows has increased from 4 to 320, that is an increase of 75 times. Daily emails increased from 12 billion to 247 billion, an increase of 20 times and the time spent online increased from 2.7 hours per week to 18 hours per week an increase of 6 times and of course we can't overlook ITunes downloads which increased from just 8 (not billion) to 10 billion. (*Newsweek*, August 2, 2010)

With all the texting going on, folks are interacting but not really communicating.

How does all this affect our ministries? Once again, I am not against technology advances. I love my iPhone, computers, and other electronic gadgets. But the important thing is knowing where the people are that we are called to minister to, and how we can best reach them with the gospel.

We have become a more visual culture rather than an auditory culture. It is easier, and we don't have to think and visualize nearly as much. Not too many years ago, we would sit by the radio and listen to all kinds of programs, everything from mysteries to comedies, sports, and news. Now we do the same type thing by sitting in front of the television or computer. Notice the effect on many churches: video screens in the sanctuary, and projecting the song lyrics on the wall. The congregation often uses a tablet or cell phone to read scriptures rather than thumbing pages in a Bible. Again, I am not saying it is good or bad, but it is a change in the reality around us, and we need to be aware of it and may need to change some of our ministry paradigms.

A somewhat weird reality shift that has occurred is that of an emotional shift. Sadness and ambiguity are the latest emotional fashions. This could affect the music style preferred in the worship service. Glenn Schellenberg of the University of Toronto studied the connection between emotions and music. "All (top 40 songs from 1960 to about 1980) published by Billboard, every single one was a major-key song. By 2009 only 18 of the (top) 40 were a major key. People are responding positively to music that has these characteristics (minor key) that are associated with negative emotions." The minor key music (22 of the top 40) is the sound of ambiguity and sadness.

This could be good or bad, but you need to be aware of what is going on in this particular area. The attitude in many churches toward ministers has changed. There's a joke that says, "Do you know why clergy are like baby diapers? They need to be changed often, and for the same reasons." Are you sure God called you into the ministry? If you are sure, then be aware the road is rough, and it will not be easy for you—but do not give up. Sometimes ministers say, "Ministry would be really great if you didn't have to deal with the people." The Great Commission's focus is on discipleship— teaching by example. What is your example teaching the people? Are you committed to finishing the course well? Only about 10 percent of ministers stay the course until age sixty-five. Please commit to being part of those who stay the course.

How can you best respond to all the paradigm changes? In general, be aware of the changes that occur, earnestly seek God's guidance for your particular situation, and carefully listen to His response. Make sure what you hear is from God. It would be wise to consult with other ministers to find out their impressions. God says there is wisdom in a multitude of counselors.

CHAPTER 9

RELATIONSHIPS

"RELATIONSHIPS HAVE THE largest impact on the brain and its growth," says Dr. David Stoop. Healthy relationships are always changing, whereas unhealthy ones never change.

The true measure of one's Christianity is his or her relationships, not his or her rituals. The single most important relationship that you have is that with your biological father. You may say, "No, the most important one is with our heavenly father." And I will say, "Your relationship with God is no better than your relationship with your dad." If you don't believe me, try this exercise. The next time you have quiet time, close your eyes and think about how you see God. I do not mean what you have been taught about God, but what He looks like to you. If you look at His face, it will most likely be your dad's face. There may be some exceptions, but they are very unusual.

You see, Dad is the first image of God that we have. In an ideal family Mom may be taking care of us and feeding us, but Dad is somewhat in the background, ideally providing for the family and protecting it. He is usually the ultimate authority in our young lives. From these images, whether good or bad, comes our image of God. In too many cases, Dad is not there for the kids, and hence they grow up feeling that God is not there for them.

A biblical passage (2 Tim. 3:1–3) that describes one indicator of the end-time and has to do with the father-child relationship is the lack of love fathers will have (hard-hearted toward kin), which stems from a term having to do with the parent-child relationship. This relationship is so important to God, and to us, that He says He will send Elijah to help turn the hearts of the fathers to the children, and the hearts of the children to the fathers, if He has to. Christ repeats this message in Luke 1:17. If God is so concerned about this relationship, shouldn't you be too? Do you ever preach on it? Have you made sure that you do not have any negative feelings toward your dad? Have you asked your kids how they feel toward you? How you feel toward your dad is the model for how your kids are to feel toward you. What we as parents do in moderation is often done in excess by our children.

> This know also, that in the last days perilous times shall come. For men shall be lovers of their own selves, covetous, boasters, proud, blasphemers, disobedient to parents, unthankful, unholy, Without natural affection, trucebreakers, false accusers, incontinent, fierce, despisers of those that are good. (2 Tim. 3:1–3)

Behold, I will send you Elijah the prophet before the coming of the great and dreadful day of the Lord: And he shall turn the heart of the fathers to the children, and the heart of the children to their fathers, lest I come and smite the earth with a curse. (Mal. 4:5–6)

And he shall go before him in the spirit and power of Elias, to turn the hearts of the fathers to the children, and the disobedient to the wisdom of the just; to make ready a people prepared for the Lord. (Luke 1:17)

This relationship with a dad is a key relationship because it affects all of our other relationships. If we have any negative feelings toward the dad, they are toward God (Luke 10:16; 1 Thess. 4:8). The Greek word translated to *despiseth* in these passages is one that means almost any negative emotion.

He that heareth you heareth me; and he that despiseth you despiseth me; and he that despiseth me despiseth him that sent me. (Luke 10:16)

He therefore that despiseth, despiseth not man, but God, who hath also given unto us his holy Spirit. (1 Thess. 4:8)

Despiseth = G0114. ἀθετέω atheteō; from a compound of 1 (as a negative particle) and a derivative of 5087; to set aside, i. e. (by implication) to disesteem, neutralize or violate: — cast off, despise, disannul, frustrate, bring to nought, reject.

AV (16)- despise 8, reject 4, bring to nothing 1, frustrate 1, disannul 1, cast off 1; to do away with, to set aside, disregard AV (2)- wicked 2; one who breaks through the restraint of law and gratifies his lusts.

A 30 -year study of 1,377 people found that the one common denominator for mental illness, hypertension, malignant tumors, coronary heart disease, and suicide was a lack of closeness (relationship) to the parents, especially the father (*Johns Hopkins Medical Journal* 134, no. 5, pp. 251–270). If this is true for our earthly father, how much more important is it for a close relationship with our heavenly Father?

"Parents are like the shuttles on a loom—they join the threads of the past to those of the future leaving their patterns on the cloth," says Dr. David Stoop.

The effects of father loss can show up in fear of commitment; professional, social, or academic failure; various addictions; great anger; and general depression. Some surveys have shown that fathers are four times more influential than mothers on children, especially in the area of spiritual things.

The child's relationship with her father is probably the most underrated and misunderstood relationship in life. It affects every other relationship in a person's life, including that with God.

Here are some of the major reactions children have to the grief of father loss.

1. Feel overly responsible and often lose their childhood

2. Feel they have to protect their mother and be ashamed of their juvenile emotions

3. Feel helpless and guilty

4. Develop various problems to distract their grief

5. Deny the pain and withdraw from reality

6. Lack of trust in authority figures, especially men

7. Tendency to abandon their own children (copy dad's behavior)

Most men and women are afraid to face their pain over their relationship with their dads because it is so painful. That gives some idea how important our relationships are. Life, and especially the Christian life, is all about relationships—with God, our family, and those around us. Christianity is not a religion; it is a personal relationship with Christ. Religions are all about rules and regulations, in other words one must earn their way to heaven by following certain rules or by doing certain good deeds. Christianity is about being part of the family of God, which is achieved by accepting Christ as our Lord and savior and being in relationship with Him.

It's not really about good deeds outweighing bad deeds or following a bunch of rules and regulations in order to go to heaven. It is about trusting Christ and what He has done for us. God does give us some commandments to enjoy a good life here on earth but they do not affect our going to heaven.

Relationships are a lot like streets: they have two sides. You are one side, and the other person is the other side. Sometimes trash builds up on one or both sides of the street, but in a relationship, you are able to clean only your side of the street. The other person is responsible for his or her side. The best way to clean your side is to forgive the other person (not behavior; God forgives us, not our sins) and to thank God for the person (1 Tim. 2:1) and what he or she did or did not do (Eph. 5:20).

> I exhort therefore, that, first of all, supplications, prayers, intercessions, and giving of thanks, be made for all men. (1 Tim. 2:1)

> Giving thanks always for all things unto God and the Father in the name of our Lord Jesus Christ. (Eph. 5:20)

One passage that shows how our human relationships affect our relationship with God is found in Mark 11:25. Christ is saying that almost any negative emotion toward anyone negatively affects our relationship with God.

And when ye stand praying, forgive, if ye have ought
against any: that your Father also which is in heaven
may forgive you your trespasses. (Mark 11:25)

In our relationship with God, He always keeps His side of the
street clean; He loves us all the time regardless of our attitude or
behavior. We still have to clean up our side of that street to keep our
relationship with Him in good order. Please do not misunderstand
what I'm saying. Once we are born into the family of God, we will
always be a part of that family. We cannot undo that relationship,
but we can make it more or less enjoyable for ourselves here on earth.

We can get out of fellowship with God, but we cannot get
out of God's family (John 10:27–29). In fact, the real you, that
person down inside you somewhere, is already just like Christ in
this world (1 John 4:17). The passage in 1 John is the fulfillment of
the promise made in Romans 8:29. We do not always behave like
Him, though. God continues to love us in spite of our behavior,
but if we misbehave, He will chasten us or let us suffer the natural
consequences of our behavior. With every decision we make, there
is a price to pay. Be sure that you are willing to pay the price before
making that decision.

My sheep hear my voice, and I know them, and they
follow me: And I give unto them eternal life; and
they shall never perish, neither shall any man pluck
them out of my hand. My Father, which gave them
me, is greater than all; and no man is able to pluck
them out of my Father's hand. (John 10:27–29)

Herein is our love made perfect, that we may have boldness in the day of judgment: because as he is, so are we in this world. (1 John 4:17)

For whom he did foreknow, he also did predestinate to be conformed to the image of his Son, that he might be the firstborn among many brethren. (Rom. 8:29)

Certainly the only relationship for salvation is the one we have with God and Christ. For that to be a right relationship, we have to accept Christ as our personal Lord and savior. For the relationship to be all that it should be, we also need to be committed to follow His leadership. The elements that make for a good relationship with God also apply to our other relationships. Some of these elements for a close relationship are that we must be committed to Him, trust Him, communicate with Him often, learn about Him, tell Him about what is going on with us (this is called "sharing"), thank Him for the many gifts He gives to us, honor Him, do not blame Him when things go astray, give Him gifts out of love rather than duty, and brag on Him to others.

Too often we hear a pastor talk about being "adopted" into the family of God. In our culture, that implies something of a second-class person or relationship, maybe even someone to be pitied. Based upon my understanding and study of the biblical use of the term, it has *nothing* to do with our term *adoption* as we normally think of it in our culture. In the New Testament, it is used only five times, once referring to our heavenly bodies. Each time it is used, it is in a book written to a Roman church. Rome had a law that required one to legally adopt his own biological children for them to get inheritance when he died. When "adopted," they were legally considered adults. This idea is reinforced in the passage related to our heavenly body (Rom. 8:23), which is part of our heavenly inheritance.

> And not only they, but ourselves also, which have the firstfruits of the Spirit, even we ourselves groan within ourselves, waiting for the adoption, to wit, the redemption of our body. (Rom. 8:23)

Under Roman law, even though they were biological children, they did not automatically receive an inheritance unless and until they had been "adopted." Paul, in using the term, was reassuring the folks in the Roman churches that they would get their heavenly inheritance. A careful study of the context in which the word is used in the New Testament shows that it is referring to our heavenly inheritance as believers. It is not about eternal life but the heavenly rewards of that life.

Once we are in a right relationship with God, let's turn our attention to human relationships and get them in order. One very common thing that interferes with our human relationships is the need to be "right." Many of us tend to feel that if we are not right, we have little or no value and are not worth loving. When we insist on being "right," we are operating independent of God; it is a focus on the self. When we are focused on the self, we are full of pride, which is living in a fantasy world. On the other hand, humbleness and humility is living in reality; they are not going around with our heads hung down, and they are not depression.

There are times when one is "right" and wants to do the right thing. This is not the same thing as feeling the need to be right in a disagreement. Sometimes in a human disagreement, we have to agree to disagree. The Bible is clear (Mark 9:50; 1 Thess. 5:13; Heb. 12:14; 1 Pet. 3:11) that God wants us to do the right thing all the time, and sometimes that is painful or can even cost us a friendship or a job.

> Finally, brethren, farewell. Be perfect, be of good comfort, be of one mind, *live in peace;* and the God of love and peace shall be with you. (2 Cor. 13:11)

> Salt is good: but if the salt have lost his saltness, wherewith will ye season it? Have salt in yourselves, and have peace one with another. (Mark 9:50)

> And to esteem them very highly in love for their work's sake. And be at peace among yourselves. (1 Thess. 5:13)

> Follow peace with all men, and holiness, without which no man shall see the Lord. (Heb. 12:14)

> Let him eschew evil, and do good; let him seek peace, and ensue it. (1 Pet. 3:11)

Would you rather be right or be in relationship? Remember that there is a difference between wanting to be right and doing what is right. Doing the right thing can be very uncomfortable or even painful at times. Christ took responsibility for everything you did wrong, and it killed Him. That does not mean He was responsible for what you did, but He took the blame and suffered the consequences for you. He did it out of love for you, and at times you have to take responsibility for the wrongdoing of someone else, because you love him or her.

Proverbs 21:2 says that every way of a man is right in his own eyes, but God considers what is in the heart. The thing that upsets us most about people who drive us up the wall is that they are showing us something about ourselves that we do not want to admit is true. Men usually have a more difficult time with a relationship with a female than women have with a relationship with a male. We see a hint of this in Genesis 2:18 when God says it is not good that man be alone. This is the only "not good" during creation week. This is partly because all males are born mentally deficient. Please do not be offended by my use of the term *deficient*. By that I mean when the male fetus is about eight to twelve weeks old, the testes have developed and begin to secrete testosterone. This testosterone washes away part of the right hemisphere of the brain—the part that deals with relationships. Also, for men there are fewer connections between the left and right hemispheres of the brain. In terms of the actual amount of brain material, males are born having a little less brain material than women.

> And the Lord God said, It is not good that the man
> should be alone; I will make him an help meet for
> him. (Gen. 2:18)

This does not mean God messed up in His design. In fact, it is part of His perfect design for men and women to become one and have an attraction to each other. This is not to say that men and women cannot function well without a spouse—they most certainly can. neither does it say that one is better than the other; they are simply different. But it does say that men and women tend to see and deal with relationships somewhat differently.

The main part of the brain loss in men is the part that deals with relationships. In one sense of the term, men do not really care about relationships as long as they are the "winner." They can learn how to do relationships correctly, but they are not born really knowing how to do so. They tend to be somewhat selfish and focus on themselves rather than on the other party.

You can observe this difference in relationship dealings in the games that little boys play versus the games that little girls play. Boy games have a winner and a loser, but girl games tend to allow all to win. Men tend to carry this into adulthood. Get two or more guys together, and if one tells some kind of story, all the others will try to one-up him. Men can learn how to do better in relationships, and that is one reason God gives us women: to help us men learn how to do it better. We can learn from other sources, but when we are married, we have to practice it for a rewarding and God-honoring marriage.

Your relationship with God or your ministry is no better than the relationship with your spouse. You may wish to disagree with me on this point, but Proverbs 16:7 tells us that when our ways please the Lord, He makes even our enemies to be at peace with us. If you are not having peace at home, check out your relationship with God. This does not mean you will not have disagreements; in fact, you will, because the two of you see the world through different eyes. But a disagreement does not have to escalate into a conflict.

Your parents' marriage (or lack thereof) is the normal blueprint for your marriage (or lack thereof). The husband-wife relationship usually reflects the husband-God relationship. Disagreements are healthy and reflect the honest expression of our individual personalities. You can disagree without being disagreeable. Very often we disagree with the way God does things. He handles such disagreement very well, but at times we do not. Conflict, on the other hand, reflects a break in the connectedness of the relationship. This is usually because neither is willing to give in or reconsider the disagreement.

The natural response to conflict is to withdraw. Healing only comes by staying in the relationship. If you do not reconnect, your negative emotions will only increase. We grow while in a relationship; this doesn't apply to only marriages. Marriage is God's relationship university. Connection requires both parties working on it. Both are hurting and have a responsibility to work on it. Conflict is God ringing your phone, and when you answer, He wants to hear you give thanks for it and ask how do He wants you to change. Think about it for a few moments. If we did not have some disagreements and conflicts, how would we ever learn to forgive and truly love? Remember that each disagreement and conflict is an opportunity to trust in God's goodness to you—another chance to grow spiritually and emotionally, as well as in relationship.

An example that I like to use is found in the book of Genesis. Genesis 2:20 states that Adam gave names to all the different animals and birds, but there was not a helpmeet for him. Why weren't any of the animals a suitable helpmeet for Adam? You might say because they couldn't talk, but we find a snake talking in the next chapter, and that did not seem to surprise Adam or Eve. Ladies please do not take this wrong, but maybe it was because none of the animals would betray, disagree with, or be cruel to Adam, and so God made Eve. Adam would never have learned to forgive or truly love with one of the animals as his helpmeet.

> And Adam gave names to all cattle, and to the fowl
> of the air, and to every beast of the field; but for
> Adam there was not found an help meet for him.
> (Gen. 2:20)

Conflict and problems are always about God wanting us to change and grow from them. If you don't learn the first time, God is merciful and will give you another opportunity to learn that lesson. As you go through your trials and are learning and growing, it affects the rest of your family, with the children paying the biggest price for your education and maturity. They do not fully understand what is going on and can develop some weird paradigms. You wind up marrying the person or ministry who will force you to grow up. Problems in your life are always about growing you, especially your faith in God's goodness.

The primary rule is that the problem is never the problem. By this, I mean what appears to be the problem is usually just a metaphor for the real problem. This is true in the family and the ministry. For example, someone comes into your office and complains about one of your messages or lessons. A good response to such a comment is, "What about the message bothers you?" Then, "Why does that bother you?" Do not defend the message or yourself. Normally that person's real issue is not with the message per se, but with something going on in his life. Another way to say it is, "Hurt people hurt people."

When someone hurts you, normally it is because she is hurting and wants you to know it. It is normally a good opportunity for you to minister to her needs. Explore with her what she is feeling as a result of the message, and ask how things are going with her and with her family.

Conflict in a marriage *always* reflects one or more of the following reasons;

The one common denominator found in all the divorces that have been studied is that the couple had stopped playing together. Tension builds between a couple over time, and the best way to release that tension is for them to laugh at themselves and each other.

Play is an excellent way for this to occur. You can even make up games if you so desire. I believe that the importance of playing is born out in Proverbs 5:18. If it were not important, why would God command us to do it?

> Let thy fountain be blessed: and rejoice with the wife of thy youth. (Prov. 5:18)

> The Hebrew term translated "rejoice" simply means to have fun, enjoy.

An old adage is, "The couple that prays together, stays together." Let me reassure you from personal experience that is not true. However, the couple that plays together, stays together. Think about it for a few moments. With whom do you like to spend time? You like to spend time with those with whom you have fun. Remember that the one common denominator among divorces is that the couple stopped playing together.

More important than a couple playing together is each one's decision to be happy with the person God gave him or her as a spouse. Where in the Bible does it say that a marriage should be happy?

Another very important source of conflict and trouble in a marriage stems from a lack of love. As we look at 2 Timothy 3:1–3, we see that in the latter days, mankind will have a lack of love. Love must be learned from someone who knows how to love. Who taught you how to love?

This know also, that in the last days perilous times shall come. For men shall be lovers of their own selves, covetous, boasters, proud, blasphemers, disobedient to parents, unthankful, unholy, Without natural affection, trucebreakers, false accusers, incontinent, fierce, despisers of those that are good. (2 Tim. 3:1–3)

"Affection" as used here is a Greek term meaning "hardhearted toward kindred." It comes from a term related to a parent-child relationship.

In today's culture. it appears that if two people are physically attracted to each other, it must be love. In my work with couples, most of which have been Christian couples, the primary cause of marital difficulties has been premarital sex. When a typical couple comes in for marital counseling, I always ask, "Why are we here?" The most frequent answers have been, "We just can't seem to communicate," or there's some kind of distrust with money: "She doesn't list the checks she writes," or "He is always charging something on the credit card."

When I hear the reason for their seeking counseling is an issue involving trust, I assume that there was premarital sex. It is humorous to watch a lot of couples and how they answer my questioning about sex. I normally ask the man, "Were the two of you physically involved prior to marriage?" Very often he will shake his head no, while at the same time she shakes her head yes.

One of my greatest surprises during my graduate work in psychology was that a textbook on marital problems written by secular psychologists would have premarital sex as the very first issue they talked about. Secular psychology is well aware of the issue of premarital sex and its negative effect on marriage, but they certainly do not advertise it (Leroy G. Baruth and Charles H. Huber, *An Introduction to Marital Theory and Therapy*).

Even unmarried couples are affected by premarital sex. They often have a tendency to argue and break up from time to time. The cause and effect are the same as with a married couple.

Premarital sex appears to affect marriage in at least two ways. One of the major ways is that it destroys the trust between two people. I think that this may be what the apostle James was talking about in James 4:1. This verse certainly describes premarital sex and its effect on a marriage and a relationship. He may not have written it for that purpose, but it is certainly applicable. When trust is broken or destroyed, the couple usually argues a lot because they do not trust what the other party says or does. They argue over money, how the children are disciplined, and everything else.

> From whence come wars and fightings among you?
> come they not hence, even of your lusts that war in
> your members? (James 4:1)

Good communication requires trust in each other. This is because we will not open up about what we really feel or think on the inside if we do not trust the other person. By the same token, we do not believe what the other person says if we do not trust them. Trust is part of the foundation of true love.

Another factor appears to be on the emotional level. It seems that on the emotional level, each person is pointing the finger at the other party and is saying, "You made me do wrong, so it is all your fault." This certainly adds to the distrust factor. We cannot undo premarital sex, but we can treat its effect on the relationship. The most effective method that I have found is to have them face each other, hold hands. and look each other in the eye. Then I have the man say (if he means it), "The premarital physical involvement was wrong, I take total responsibility for it, and I ask for your forgiveness." Hopefully she agrees to forgive him. Then I have her say and mean the same thing to him. I ask each one what that experience was like for them. The woman normally gets a lot of relief from doing the exercise. Complete healing of the relationship will take some time after doing the exercise because healing is a process.

Either party may have been responsible for the premarital sex, but by each accepting full responsibility for it, that means they quit blaming each other. In addition, it is an act of true love. That is what Christ did for you: He took responsibility for everything you do wrong. The term *responsibility* as I am using it here does not mean the party caused the action, but rather takes the blame (responsibility) for it and pays the price.

Please note that in most disagreements and conflict, there is a natural tendency to blame the other person. The solution requires each to take personal responsibility for his or her behavior, ask for forgiveness, and give forgiveness. This helps each person emotionally feel better toward the other person, and it begins a new trusting process. Forgiveness is not a one-time thing; it is a process and takes time. We often have to wear out the emotions involved. We cannot change the facts, but we can change the feelings.

Even secular psychologists recognize that there is a connection between our sexuality and our spirituality. Some say, "Spirituality and sexuality sleep in the bed and you cannot awaken one without awakening the other"(M. Scott Peck).

The first evidence of sin in the lives of mankind apparently showed up in the sexual organs (Gen. 3:7). Why? Perhaps it's to remind mankind that the source of life had been polluted. What do aprons cover up? They normally cover the sexual organs. This alone shows us that there is a close connection between sexuality and spirituality. God even used man's sexuality (circumcision) as a sign of His covenant with the children of Israel (Gen. 17:11).

> And the eyes of them both were opened, and they knew that they were naked; and they sewed fig leaves together, and made themselves aprons. (Gen. 3:7)

> And ye shall circumcise the flesh of your foreskin; and it shall be a token of the covenant betwixt me and you. (Gen. 17:11)

Notice that in the Garden of Eden, the knowledge of good and evil grows from the same roots and bears fruit on the same tree. There was one fruit, and whether it was the knowledge of good or evil usually depends on how you choose to look at the problem. In much the same way, your marriage can bear good or bad fruit; they both come from the same roots. Your differences can be used to build a good relationship or a bad one—the choice is yours. My use of *differences* here means men are different from women; we see the world through different eyes and may even define words differently. Another way to express my idea is the old saying "Two heads are better than one." Certainly, one way to have a much better relationship with each other is to not partake of the tree of the knowledge of good and evil. For us, that means to not begin to judge (condemn) each other or our motives. Once we begin the judging process, the relationship suffers. We normally begin the judging process at the point we feel that God is not being good to us in this relationship. *Never* start thinking that you made a mistake by marrying that person. If you do, you are saying that God goofed and is not good to you.

Every marriage has grounds for divorce before the wedding ceremony is over. Think about it: during the courting process, we are usually on our best behavior in our appearance and manners, but that is usually presenting a false image of what we are really like. For instance, before marriage the guy usually offers to get her some tea or a Coke, but afterward he asks her to bring him a tea or Coke while he watches television. He probably never saw her with her hair in curlers. We usually marry someone with the same basic issues that we have, but theirs is often exhibited in a different manner than ours. We apparently recognize this similarity on the emotional level rather than on the cognitive level. This may well be the real attraction factor, because we feel that others can understand us because they have the same basic issues.

It is not uncommon for guys to marry someone like their mom, and for girls to marry someone like their dad. By this I mean we tend to marry a person with the same basic issues as our opposite sex parent. Where did we get our issues? From our parents! I do not believe any of us marry for the right reason. There may be one or two exceptions, but I doubt it. The right reason to marry is to glorify God (1 Cor. 10:31). I bet that you did not marry for that reason.

> Whether therefore ye eat, or drink, or whatsoever ye
> do, do all to the glory of God. (1 Cor. 10:31)

Marriage is not meant to satisfy all of your emotional needs—God does that (Phil. 4:19). He may use the Bible, another person, a job, or maybe even a pet as part of that process.

> But my God shall supply all your need according to
> his riches in glory by Christ Jesus. (Phil. 4:19)

Women tend to become the way that they are treated. Some writers (Gary Smalley) say that if you have been married five years, your wife has become the way she has been treated. Women respond to the way they are treated probably more so than men. Men are to treat their wives as very delicate, very valuable vases (1 Pet. 3:7). It is not all one-sided; when the husband is not doing right, God promises to change him if she demonstrates love in spite of him and his behavior (1 Pet. 3:1). God does not put a time limit on it, so it may take a long time.

> Likewise, ye husbands, dwell with them according to knowledge, giving honour unto the wife, as unto the weaker vessel, and as being heirs together of the grace of life; that your prayers be not hindered. (1 Pet. 3:7)

> Likewise, ye wives, be in subjection to your own husbands; that, if any obey not the word, they also may without the word be won by the conversation of the wives. (1 Pet. 3:1)

Marriage is God's relationship university. God intends for us to learn how to love (which also involves forgiving) people even though we have disagreements or conflicts with them. Not only by our disagreements but also by our other differences like how a woman views the home as opposed to how a man sees it. Normally the woman tends to view the home as an expression of her personality, whereas men tend to express their personalities on the job. Women are to be in complete control of the home (1 Tim. 5:14). In this passage, the term "guide the house" is a translation of the Greek *oikodespoteo*. This term literally means house (*oiko*) absolute total ruler (*despoteo* = despot). In our culture, that means she can control the TV programs watched, furniture arrangement, decorations and more. Men can live in a home without curtains, knickknacks, and flower vases, but women usually feel a need for them. How you choose to deal with all these differences can either improve or worsen the relationship.

> I will therefore that the younger women marry, bear children, guide the house, give none occasion to the adversary to speak reproachfully. (1 Tim. 5:14)

> > "Guide the house" as mentioned earlier, is a Greek term which means "house despot" or absolute ruler of the home.

Many of us go into the marriage relationship with unrealistic expectations. In fact, most of us have an unwritten agenda or contract that we expect our spouse to fulfill, but we have never told them what our real expectations are. Then we get upset with them when they do not fulfill our agenda or contract. If it bugs you, it is your problem.

By nature we tend to grow apart (Isa. 53:6), with each going his or her own way. For the marriage relationship to be what God intended, we have to work at it all of our lives. If we simply coast, we will grow apart. There is no such thing as "marriage problems." Marriage does *not* cause problems—it simply brings problems to the surface that each party brought into the marriage.

> All we like sheep have gone astray; we have *turned every one to his own way;* and the Lord hath laid on him the iniquity of us all. (Isa. 53:6)

Complaining is the adult's way of crying to get one's way. Problems are always about God wanting to change us and not necessarily the other person. If He wants the other person changed, let Him do it. He may or may not want your help. Remember that when you mistreat your Christian spouse, you will have to answer to the father.

> Yet ye say, Wherefore? *Because the LORD hath been witness between thee and the wife of thy youth, against whom thou hast dealt treacherously:* yet is she thy companion, and the wife of thy covenant. (Mal. 2:14)

What is God's purpose for marriage? The primary purpose is to glorify God. Another one is using your spouse to knock off your rough edges, to demonstrate God's love for and relationship with His people, and to create children, His university for learning how to have a relationship.

Romance versus Love

One of the grossest misrepresentations rampant in our culture today is that of what love is. The public is taught, and in general believes, that romance and love are the same thing. If you feel romantic toward someone, then you must be "in love" with them. Nothing could be further from the truth.

Love is a conscious decision. We do not "fall in love"—we must choose to love. On the other hand, romantic feelings (sometimes referred to as infatuation) are often just a desire to have sex with the object of those feelings, or to be physically close to them. For example, take any of the great love stories, like Romeo and Juliet. Notice that every time they tried to get together, Juliet's father would interfere—hence the great romantic and infatuation feelings. This is perhaps wanting to have sex but not being able to do so, or to become one with the other person, or simply be with him or her. That is one reason why normally when a couple first gets married, they have very frequent sex, but as time goes on the frequency diminishes. The sexual desire is being satisfied, so the romantic and infatuation feelings begin to disappear.

When people have sex before or outside of marriage, very often they will feel guilty, and in order to avoid that feeling, they will tell themselves that they are "in love" with the person. There is currently some idea floating around that if you "love" someone, then sex is okay even if not married. In our culture today, sex is often engaged in without romantic or infatuation feelings. Some try to convince you that it is simply another physical need, like hunger or thirst, and that it is okay to satisfy that need any way you can; it means nothing more than that.

The reality is that sex is very much more than a physical need. It forms an emotional and spiritual bond. Consider two things in the following passage: First, how a married couple becomes "one flesh." Second, "Christ and the church." It is a great mystery how man and woman become one flesh, and how Christ and the church become one.

For this cause shall a man leave his father and mother, and shall be joined unto his wife, and they two shall be one flesh. This is a great mystery: but I speak concerning Christ and the church. (1 Cor. 5:31–32)

Consider 1 Corinthians 6:16–17. "What? know ye not that he which is joined to an harlot is one body? for two, saith he, shall be one flesh. But he that is joined unto the Lord is one spirit." Sex unites in several ways the two people. This may seem a little (or a lot) far out but, not in 1 Corinthians 5:32 and 1 Corinthians 6:17. The connection between Christ and believers is apparently spoken of in a sexual context. Is there some kind of spiritual sexual connection? Don't go overboard with this idea; it is simply something for you to think about and study, if you so desire.

The whole point is that there is much more to sex than a physical need. That is one reason why the experts on sexual abuse tell us that sexual abuse goes all the way to the spirit and requires spiritual medicine to heal. This is from secular psychologists. This is spoken of in-house but is not advertised to the public.

The best definition of love that I have found is, "Love is doing what is best for the spiritual growth of the object of that love" (M. Scott Peck). Although this definition is consistent with the Bible, there is a dangerous area here, especially for ministers. The author of that definition of love also points out that "love and spirituality sleep in the same bed and you cannot awaken one without awakening the other." This may be why some ministers fall into affairs.

One example is where a male minister leads a female to Christ. This generally arouses a number of positive emotions in each party, which might be interpreted by one or the other as "love" or great appreciation. A very important rule in this situation, or in any situation where a male minister counsels a woman, is that the minister must not express his emotions to the woman. She can express all of hers to him, but not the other way around. When the man expresses his emotions to a woman, there is usually an emotional connection established between the two parties, especially on the woman's part. This rule is more important and effective than an open door when counseling, a window in your office door, or a secretary just outside your office.

If you are a man counseling with a woman, there is a critical rule to follow if you wish to avoid temptation and inappropriate behavior, as well as any appearance of evil. You may have heard or read that the safest way to counsel is have your office door open while counseling, to have a secretary outside your office, or to have a small window in your office door. None of these things work! They may help but are not the ultimate protection.

The secret is that it is okay for a female to express to a male all of her emotions and events going on in her life, but if you (a male) express your emotions to a female counselee and or tell about your relationships, you have crossed the line. This is because when you share with the female counselee, there is usually an emotional bond that takes place, and it is just one small step from there to inappropriate behavior. Out of empathy, you may feel like sharing, but do not do it. In addition, there are women who intentionally try to cause ministers to fall morally. You do not need this kind of stress, so don't take any chances.

As I have already mentioned, men are born missing the part of the brain that deals with relationships. About the only way the natural man knows how to have a relationship ("be one") with a woman, unless he has learned otherwise, is via sex, a physical relationship. Even when married, if a man gets his meals on time and has sex whenever he wants it, he says and thinks the relationship is great—but the wife may very well be dying emotionally on the inside.

The need to be right is probably one of the largest obstacles to a great relationship. Men, because of their secret fear (I am not a real man), usually feel the need to be right in order to prove they are real men, and that causes arguments. An excellent relationship question is, "Would you rather be right or be in relationship?"

Women usually desire, and need, lots of affection; that helps them feel more secure. Several hugs each day normally helps keep the relationship on track.

Another area of potential discord is that of not speaking your partner's "love language." It appears that each of us feels more loved when we are communicated with in our love language. There are five love languages (Gary Smalley, *The Five Love Languages*), and they are non-sexual touch, acts of service, affirming words, spending quality time, and gifts. We rarely marry a person with the same love language as ours. As men, we have to express love in our wives' love language for them to feel loved by us. The more they express love to us in our love language, the more loved we feel by her.

As we study marriages, there appear to be some five different stages that they usually go through. The first stage is termed the honeymoon stage. The term is very meaningful because it expresses the idea that the relationship is sweet as honey, but it doesn't usually last longer than a month (one moon) or so. Then we begin to transition into the power struggle stage. This is where we determine whether the toilet tissue rolls off the top or bottom of the roll, whether we squeeze the toothpaste tube in the middle or bottom, and the like. There is often a struggle to finally decide who will be doing which jobs, and how they will be done around the house and bank account. Some couples are married fifty years and are still in the power struggle stage.

The proper way we get out of the power struggle stage is to apply the principles of true love to the relationship (application stage). This means forgiving, showing love and acceptance, respect, putting the other party first, and more. The more we apply the principles and the longer we apply them, the more the marriage relationship begins to change for the better (transition stage). You should continue applying the principles of real love till you eventually reach the true love stage. Even when we reach that stage, it does not mean we stay there. We can fall back to the power struggle stage at any time, and we frequently do. If that happens, we have to restart applying the principles of true love to the relationship. We have to work on our relationship all of our lives.

These stages and principles apply to our ministry as well. When we go to a new church or position, there is hopefully a honeymoon period, and then starts the power struggle. We really need to apply true love for God, for our calling, and for the people. We can fall back to the power struggle stage at any time, so we need to stay alert and steady in our love.

Guidelines for Improving Your Marriage

1. Put Christ and His will first in your life and marriage. Among other things, this means to sacrifice your desires for your spouse and what he or she desires. Put the other person ahead of yourself in the relationship.

2. Remember that you made a commitment for better and for worse, so if you get worse, that is what you signed up for. Thank God for it and ask Him how He wants you to change.

3. Ministers are to put their families ahead of their ministry. Your ministry will be no better than your marriage, and God says family should be first after Him. If you are not

ministering to your family, you are not qualified to minister to anyone else.

> For if a man know not how to rule (to stand before, i. e. (in rank) to preside, or (by implication) to practice: maintain) his own house, how shall he take care of the church of God? (1 Tim. 3:5)

4. Men, God will speak to you through your wife more than any other way. Listen to her!

5. Become each other's greatest source of fulfillment and recreational companionship. This is how you do it: play with each other often.

6. Avoid being the source of each other's unhappiness.

7. Create a lifestyle that both of you enjoy.

8. Never make a major decision without your spouse's enthusiastic agreement.

9. Men, you need to learn to love your wives as Christ loved the church (Eph. 5:25). How did Jesus love the church? He sacrificed His desires for her needs, gave of Himself, communicated, and even gave His life.

> Husbands, love your wives, even as Christ also loved the church, and gave himself for it. (Eph. 5:25)

10. Men, take full responsibility for everything that goes wrong. Christ did that for the church (including you), and you should do the same for your wife because it is the loving thing to do. It does not mean you are the cause of the situation, but you accept that responsibility (take the blame and pay the price) because you love that person.

11. Men, express your emotions to your wife. When you do, it makes her feel more secure and much closer to you (women in general are basically insecure).

12. Women, love your husband by showing him your admiration and respect. That is what helps him feel loved by you.

    Nevertheless let every one of you in particular so love his wife even as himself; and the wife see that she reverence her husband. (Eph. 5:33)

13. Trust each other. It is a conscious decision and is not earned—it is given. Trust in God to do what is best for you.

14. If you disrespect or disregard each other, you are putting down the very image of God, especially if both of you are Christians.

Every time your spouse offends you:

1. That is a message from God saying He wants you to change something

2. Thank God for the offense.

    Giving thanks always for all things unto God and
    the Father in the name of our Lord Jesus Christ.
    (Eph. 5:20)

3. Ask God what He wants you to change or learn.

4. Forgive your spouse. Forgiveness is always for the person,
    not the behavior.

5. Find out what your spouse's feelings are at the time. She
    may begin by talking about what you have or have not done.
    Simply agree with her and say something like, "But what are
    your feelings right now?"

The secret of a smooth landing is finding the right attitude in
spite of the atmospheric conditions. What kind of relationship with
yourself do you have? I will discuss that in the next chapter.

CHAPTER 10

IDENTITY

WHAT IS YOUR relationship with yourself? By this, I mean how do you see yourself? Do you like or love yourself? If not, why not? Do you see yourself as having any real value? Do you have real value as a person, a human being? How you answer affects your whole life, your family's lives, and your ministry.

How much are you, as a person, worth? Where do you get your self-worth? Or perhaps I should ask, do you get it from your own personal approval, your identity, your performance, or something else? Be very honest and introspective in your answer. Where you get it becomes an object of worship for you.

Do you ever pretend to be someone or something that you are not? Why do you do that? Why aren't you happy with who you really are?

Do you strive for acceptance and approval? Whose approval are you seeking—God's, your dad's, your congregation's, your spouse's? Why? Whom do you turn to in a crisis?

Examine yourselves, whether ye be in the faith; prove your own selves. Know ye not your own selves, how that Jesus Christ is in you, except ye be reprobates? (2 Cor. 13:5)

For as he thinketh in his heart, so is he. (Prov. 23:7)

Wherefore let him that thinketh he standeth take heed lest he fall. (1 Cor. 10:12)

Your answers to the preceding questions tell a lot about whether or not you really believe what God says about you. First of all, God said you were worth suffering and dying for; that means you have tremendous value as a person. How much more valuable could you be? If you do not really believe what God says about you, you are teaching your people to not fully believe God and His word by your example.

In ministry we often hear and talk about the world system. We often hear the term used to mean the way the world in general thinks and acts, as opposed to God's way. One of the primary things the world system teaches us, or tries to teach us, is that a person is worth only as much as you can produce or what you own. Being of Scotch heritage and having a lot of mathematics in my education, I have boiled this down to a simple equation: You= $ or U=$.

In other words, the world system says you are worth the size of your paycheck or the size of your ministry, or how many amens you received during your last sermon. Another way of saying it is, "You must be successful in order to be lovable." If you have bought into this idea, you are not using God's measure of success. Or as Dr. Phil McGraw would say, "How's that working for you?"

All of us seem to start out with the idea that "If you knew the real me (the real person down inside somewhere), you would not love me." We get that message from many different sources as we grow up, like a teacher who says, "Why can't you make grades like the other kids?" Or maybe a parent says, "Why aren't you more like your brother?" Certainly we get it from other kids when they don't choose us for their team, call us names, or tease us about having glasses or being overweight. We tend to interpret these messages that way because there must be something wrong with me. That interpretation means "I am unlovable. I am not worth anything."

As ministers, we need to keep in mind what Paul says in Galatians 1:10. "For if I yet pleased men, I should not be the servant of Christ." He is saying that we should not be seeking the approval of men, but of Christ, by what we do and how we do it. For example, how do you judge whether you brought a good message or sermon? Is it by how many amens you get or how many negative responses you get? On the other hand, how does God judge if you did a good job? God gives you an A+ if you did what He wanted you to do out of love for Him and the people, and with a right attitude. He looks at both your obedience and attitude. Take a look at the priest mentioned in 2 Chronicles 25:2.

And he did that which was right in the sight of the
Lord, but not with a perfect heart.

The world system is at the heart of the "salvation by works" mindset.
This idea is that you must "earn" salvation by your good works, and
you have to keep doing good works to keep your salvation and God's
love. The emphasis is on what the individual can or must do, rather
than what Jesus has already done for us. Many churches use this world
system with a Christian whitewash. They emphasize performance as
the measure of value, along with importing organizational structures
and procedures from the world, while putting a Christian label on
them. There is no small wonder that so many churches maintain the
"salvation by works" mindset.

Do you love God more for what He does or for who He is?
Which do you think He loves you for, what you do or who you are?
Do you perform out of love or to get God to love you? Please do not
get caught up in the Martha Syndrome.

Remember how Mary and Martha threw a party, and Jesus and
the disciples were there. Martha was running around and making
sure everyone had food, drink, or whatever, working her fingers to
the bone. She happened to look over in the corner and saw her sister
sitting on her duff and doing nothing. Man, did she get hacked off.
She walks over to Jesus and complains about her sister not helping.
Jesus tells her that Mary is doing what is important: nothing but
spending time with Him. Which of these ladies is your role model
for your ministry?

Are you trying to take care of everyone's needs and desires and not resting with Jesus? Why are you doing that? Your people need the Lord much more than they need you. Set the right example for them; that is the way we teach true discipleship. You need to spend time with Jesus, not just doing ministry to or for others. When is your Sabbath, your vacation? God took time out from creation, so why can't you do the same? You might say that Satan never takes a day off. That is true, but who do you want as your role model, God or Satan?

Just what makes a good Christian? Does it mean doing good deeds or spending quality time with Jesus? It is not about what we can do, but what we let Christ do through us, and that does not happen without spending time with Him. One very important way of showing love to anyone is by spending time with them. If we truly love Jesus, we will spend time with Him.

Salvation by grace is given lip service by many ministers and believers, but it's not really believed. It is easy to accept Christ but not always easy to believe His words. Take a very short test: Do you believe the Bible—the whole Bible? What about Proverbs 12:21?

> There shall no evil happen to the just but the wicked shall be filled with mischief. (Prov. 12:21)

Well, did you pass that test? Most Christians accept God's salvation through Christ, but not His love. Do you really feel loved by God, or do you simply believe that you are loved by Him? We normally feel like we have to earn His love because of the world system's teachings. We tend to forget that love is always given but never earned. Love requires time and attention. Are you spending quality time with God? Quality time is always found in the midst of quantity time.

One passage of scripture that I find is often misinterpreted is John 8:32. We like to say it talks about being free from sin, but if you study the context, it is spoken to believers that when they know the truth, they will be free from having to perform to get God's love. It goes along with Galatians 5:1 and Ephesians 2:8. Quit huffing and puffing, trying to impress God with your good works; quit trying to earn brownie points with Him. Simply do what He tells you and in the way He tells you to do it.

> And ye shall know the truth, and the truth shall make you free. (John 8:32)

> Stand fast therefore in the liberty wherewith Christ hath made us free, and be not entangled again with the yoke of bondage. (Gal. 5:1)

> For by grace are ye saved through faith; and that not of yourselves: *it is the gift of God*. (Eph. 2:8)

A word of caution: If you do not love yourself, you cannot really accept love from anyone else (including God), or feel it. If you are a believer, the real you is already just like Christ (1 John 4:17). That means you do not really love Christ if you do not love yourself (the real you).

> Herein is our love made perfect, that we may have
> boldness in the day of judgment: because *as he is, so
> are we in this world.* (1 John 4:17)

As you minister and evaluate your ministry, keep in mind, "Where does it say God is interested in numbers, other than the number one?" God is more concerned with making disciples than increasing the number, per ce, of church members. He does want to see more folks saved. We only teach by example, so what is your personal example in teaching your folks? If we disciple our people, they will be better witnesses, and we probably will see an increase in members in our ministry. God places those in the church as He sees fit (1 Cor. 12:18). Whose job is it to motivate the people, yours or the Holy Spirit's? Whose job does God say it is? When you try to motivate people in your own strength, you risk burning out because you are not equipped to do the Holy Spirit's job.

> But now hath God set the members every one of them
> in the body, as it hath pleased him. (1 Cor. 12:18)

If you think that I am off base with where you are with the world system, take this little test. List six things that are wrong with you. That is the whole test. If you list anything, it will always be "performance" and not the real you. Born-again believers have nothing wrong with them and cannot honestly name anything that is not performance. Some examples of the things we normally list are worry, impatience, being unwise in our decisions, fear, and being disorganized. These are all things we do, not things wrong with our real person.

You see, freedom from having to perform is the abundant life. This is resting in Christ, and He did it all for us. Some references are, Hebrews 4:3, 9–10. On the other hand, we can be very active, do everything just right, and yet not have a good relationship with God, as I mentioned earlier.

> Come unto me, all ye that labour and are heavy laden, and I will give you rest. Take my yoke upon you, and learn of me; for I am meek and lowly in heart: and ye shall find rest unto your souls. For my yoke is easy, and my burden is light. (Matt. 11:28–30)

> For we which have believed do enter into rest, as he said, As I have sworn in my wrath, if they shall enter into my rest: although *the works were finished from the foundation of the world*. (Heb. 4:3)

> There remaineth therefore a rest to the people of God. For he that is entered into his rest, he also *hath ceased from his own works*, as God did from his. (Heb. 4:9–10)

> And he did that which was right in the sight of the Lord, but *not with a perfect heart*. (2 Chron. 25:2)

We as ministers also feed into the world system at times by using the phrase "sinners saved by grace" too freely and in the wrong context. That phrase describes how we got saved, but it does not describe who we are now. God does not refer to us as sinners saved by grace, but as His children, saints, royal priests, peculiar people, and the elect.

The born-again believers are already pure. Christ and the Holy Spirit have already done the work. We have been made partakers of Christ's divine nature (2 Pet. 1:4). Can a person have two natures? Absolutely not! If you have two natures, which one is the real you? We are still in the flesh, which wants to sin, but that is not our nature (2 Cor. 5:17). It is simply something that we have to wrestle with, but it is not our nature. Because "all things are made new," there is no room for two natures (Eph. 2:15). We are "perfect" spirits (Heb. 12:23). This passage is written to living saints, not dead ones. What changes would occur if you started seeing your spouse in this way? What about seeing yourself, your staff, your deacons, your elders, your field supervisor, and your parents this way?

> *Now ye are clean* through the word which I have spoken unto you. (John 15:3)

> And *ye are complete* in him, which is the head of all principality and power. (Col. 2:10)

> Purge out therefore the old leaven, that ye may be a new lump, as *ye are unleavened*. For even Christ our Passover is sacrificed for us. (1 Cor. 5:7)

> And such were some of you: but *ye are washed*, but *ye are sanctified*, but ye are justified in the name of the Lord Jesus, and *by the Spirit* of our God. (1 Cor. 6:11)

> By the which will *we are sanctified* through the offering of the body of Jesus Christ once for all ...

For by one offering *he hath perfected for ever* them that are sanctified. (Heb. 10:10, 14)

I in them, and thou in me, that *they may be made perfect in one*; and that the world may know that thou hast sent me, and hast loved them, as thou hast loved me ... And I have declared unto them thy name, and will declare it: that the love wherewith thou hast loved me may be in them, and *I in them*. (John 17:23, 26)

For whom he did foreknow, he also did *predestinate to be conformed to the image of his Son*, that he might be the firstborn among many brethren. (Rom. 8:29)

For he hath made him to be sin for us, who knew no sin; *that we might be made the righteousness of God in him*. (2 Cor. 5:21)

As the previous verses show, we are already clean, complete, and unleavened. What is *leaven* symbolic of? Sin. In fact, we are already just like Christ right now in this present world (1 John 4:17; John 17:23, 26). This passage fulfills the promise made in Romans 8:29 and 2 Corinthians 5:21.

I wish to digress a moment her to clarify something. Notice the use of the term *predestinate* in Romans 8:29. The term is not used to predestinate one's salvation, but rather to predestine that believers will be made just like Christ and become one of His brothers or sisters. Because this is the reality of our salvation, God actually says this about you, "Thou art my beloved Son/daughter, in thee

I am well pleased" (Luke 3:22; Mark 1:11; Matt. 3:17). That does not mean that God is always pleased with our behavior, but He is pleased with us. This is all about our real identity, who we really are. Are you willing to believe what God says about who you really are?

> And lo a voice from heaven, saying, This is my beloved Son, *in whom I am well pleased.* (Matt. 3:17)

> And there came a voice from heaven, saying, Thou art my beloved Son, *in whom I am well pleased.* (Mark 1:11)

> And the Holy Ghost descended in a bodily shape like a dove upon him, and a voice came from heaven, which said, Thou art my beloved Son; *in thee I am well pleased.* (Luke 3:22)

If you really believe what God says about you, then you can verbalize the following quotation with gusto.

> I confess, I am an awesome spirit being of magnificent worth as a person. I am deeply loved of God, I am fully pleasing to God, I am absolutely complete in Christ. And when my person is expressed through my performance, the reflection is dynamically unique. There has never been another like me in the history of mankind, nor will there ever be. I am an original, one of a kind, really somebody and so are you! (Dr. James Mahoney)

CHAPTER 11

TRUTH

JUST WHAT IS truth? John 14:6 states, "Jesus saith unto him, I am the way, the truth, and the life: no man cometh unto the Father, but by me." We find this repeated in John 8:32—"And ye shall know the truth, and the truth shall make you free."

These verses tell us that "real truth" is a person, Jesus Christ. Real truth is not a set of propositions, but a person. Real freedom is found in a right relationship with that person. A right relationship with Christ requires us to know and recognize the difference between truth and error (untruth) in our thinking, our world view, and the way we see ourselves and others.

Years ago, an agnostic Russian philosopher was working on defining truth. He came up with this definition: "Truth is an accurate representation of that which is under consideration, and its relationship to all things past, present and future." He realized that with this definition, only an infinite mind could know the truth. That requires a God, and so he became a believer. The only aspect of truth that we can know is what the infinite mind chooses to reveal to us.

So how do we know anything? How do we know what we don't know? To answer these questions, we have to explore the dynamics of knowing. We have experiences happening to and around us all the time. An experience is what happens without any meaning attached to it. We normally attach a meaning to an experience right away. For example, we experience the temperature of the room, and then we decide if we think the temperature is too warm, too cool, or just right. We often attach meaning to an experience without any reexamination.

We tend to choose our friends from those folks who have the same general interpretations that we do ("they think like I do"). Once we attach a meaning to the experience, it becomes our reality, our truth. Truth, as I determine it, is in reality just my concept of truth, my interpretation, my understanding.

"Don't make the mistake of believing that you have all the truth," says Rev. Jack Haford. In addition, do not make the mistake of presenting *a* truth as *the* truth.

History as I know it is simply a compilation of my truth. It shapes my interpretation of future experiences. For example, have you ever found a coin in a pay phone or vending machine? If you have, you probably keep checking pay phones or vending machines for more coins. By the same token, my truth becomes the box in which I put various people. It is the lens through which I view the world and those in it.

My truth (my experiences plus my interpretation of them) is the greatest enemy of faith. For example, the communists in Russia used to tell the schoolchildren to pray for some candy. The kids did not get any candy, and the leaders would tell them the next day, "See? There is no God." We tend to forget that God answers our prayers with yes, no, or "wait."

My truth is shaped by what is in my personal belief system (PBS). The term used in the Bible for the PBS is the heart. For example:

> But those things which proceed out of the mouth come forth from the heart; and they defile the man. For out of the heart proceed evil thoughts, murders, adulteries, fornications, thefts, false witness, blasphemies. (Matt. 15:18–19)

Notice that the beliefs in the PBS determines your thinking. Your PBS began to be developed *before* you were born; a majority of it was complete by about age ten. Some examples of these beliefs are: "life should be fair," "I must be right," "if you knew the real me, you would not love me," "I deserve to be happy," and "I should get what I want." The PBS has both true and false beliefs.

A false belief is a belief that is an error, that isn't true. A true belief is a belief that is true. Part of maturing spiritually and emotionally is to replace the false beliefs (error) with true beliefs. Our false beliefs normally appear to fall into four general categories: performance, approval, punishment, and control.

The category of performance is identified by the belief or feeling that "my performance determines my worth/value as a person." In other words, it is the belief that I have to meet certain standards of performance before I can feel good about myself, or before anyone else can feel good about me. This is the basis of the salvation by works concept and expresses the world system, which says you are worth only what you can produce. A simplified equation of this concept is U = $.

This false belief category creates the "fear of failure" syndrome. This in turn causes one to be self-critical, become a perfectionist so one will not fail, have a tendency to manipulate others, and usually avoid certain activities for fear of failure.

The category of approval has the belief or feeling that "my performance must be accepted and approved by others before I can feel good about myself." It tends to create the "fear of rejection" syndrome. This syndrome can show up as one being shy and unsociable, being critical of others, withdrawing to avoid disapproval, and being depressed when criticized.

The punishment category believes or feels that "those whose performance is not acceptable are not worthy of love and must be blamed and punished." The fear of punishment syndrome is evidenced by believing that when things go wrong, it must be God punishing me, being afraid of what God might do to me, having to tell others when they are wrong, having a tendency to always blame others, going on a lot of guilt trips, and usually having a very dry spiritual life.

The basic belief or feeling of the control category is that "I am no better than my performance, which is not very good. Therefore something must be wrong with me, and I am unable to change myself. I am hopeless unless I am in control." This category is evidenced by the "shame" syndrome. This syndrome results in one repeatedly thinking of past failures, feeling like one continues to repeat certain mistakes, feeling inferior, having a tendency to engage in destructive habits, and feeling one will never have a complete and wonderful life.

A primary rule to keep in mind is, "Do not let others, other than God, determine the truth about you."

CHAPTER 12

FORGIVENESS

THE MOST IMPORTANT concept in Christianity, and probably one of the most misunderstood, is that of forgiveness. Without forgiveness, there is no salvation. There are several reasons why the concept of forgiveness is misunderstood. First of all, it is a divine concept, and we humans have difficulty fully understanding divine concepts because of our finite minds. Another reason is that many of us have not taken the time or effort to do a careful study of forgiveness. Still another reason for the misunderstanding is we do not make the proper distinction between forgiveness and unforgiveness. You see, we often diminish our unforgiveness and feel like we have forgiven. Unforgiveness is like you drinking poison and expecting the other person to die.

One of the big hindrances to being more forgiving is our emotions when we have been offended, or at least when we feel offended. Our natural (fleshly) reaction is to desire revenge of some type. Then at times we think, "I can't ever forgive them for doing that," or even, "I can't ever forgive myself for doing that."

"Forgiveness then, involves three elements: injury, a debt resulting from the injury, and a cancellation of the debt." (Charles Stanley, *Forgiveness*).

I love Mark Twain's statement about forgiveness: "Forgiveness is the fragrance that the violet sheds on the heel that has crushed it." Christ said, "Forgive us our debts as we forgive our debtors" (Matt. 6:12). How one responds to a given situation says a lot about how one views God and other human beings. This is a major part of one's worldview, one's paradigms.

One of the points that Christ is making is that our vertical relationship with God is much more related to our horizontal relationships with those around us than we would like to admit. "Forgiveness is for-giving to others." Unforgiveness negatively affects our real relationship with God, but not His relationship with us.

There are a number of misconceptions or myths about forgiveness. One results from the most frequently used Greek word for forgiveness in the New Testament, *aphemi*, which simply means "to let go." This myth says that is all there is to it.

Another myth presented (Augsberger, 1981) states that forgiveness involves letting go of all negative feelings and restoring trust. This is an abusive interpretation for victims of abuse and could subject them to even more abuse. You see, as a general rule, we cannot restore trust until we are able to see a real change in the offender. An interesting passage to study is Luke 17:3. "Take heed to yourselves: If thy brother trespass against thee, rebuke him; and if he repent, forgive him." Notice the part that says, "if he repent." If he repents, we are to forgive, but if he doesn't, the implication is that we cannot restore the relationship.

A third myth is presented in the *Anchor Bible Dictionary*, which summarizes forgiveness as wiping out an offense from one's memory. First of all, with this definition, if we have been deeply hurt by someone, we cannot wipe that out of our memory. Only God can wipe wrongdoings from His memory; we can't always do so. This approach avoids real forgiveness altogether.

Another important aspect of forgiveness is the physical ramifications of not forgiving.

> Our research shows that simply thinking about one's offender in a begrudging way can have immediate physical ramifications. Short, fleeting thoughts are unlikely to have long-term health impact, but we know hostility is a potent risk factor for heart disease. When we have deep wounds, and hostility becomes an engrained personality trait, then it can be health eroding.(Charlotte Witvliet).

When we do not forgive, we become losers.

One of the reasons forgiveness is so difficult to do is because forgiveness is a divine concept and requires faith. What is the one thing that caused the disciples to ask for more faith?

> Take heed to yourselves: If thy brother trespass against thee, rebuke him; and if he repent, forgive him. And if he trespass against thee seven times in a day, and seven times in a day turn again to thee, saying, I repent; thou shalt forgive him. *And the apostles said unto the Lord, Increase our faith.* (Luke 17:3–5)

Why did they ask for more faith? Seeing many miracles did not increase their faith, but the instruction to forgive caused them to realize that they needed more faith. It takes more faith to forgive than to believe in miracles. One main reason is that we usually cannot see or feel God's goodness when we are in pain.

Christ promised us that offenses would come into our lives. There are two classes of offended folks: those who have been offended, and those who think they have been offended. Which class are you in? You are probably in both. Every offense that we experience is an opportunity to grow spiritually. We grow when we trust God even when we don't want to. It is a conscious decision.

> Then said he unto the disciples, it is impossible but that offenses will come: but woe unto him, through whom they come. (Luke 17:1)

Forgiveness is *always for the person* and not the deed. God forgave us, not our sins. Sin is sin, and He buries it in the deepest part of the sea. If our sin was forgiven, why did He have to bury it? Notice what is stated in the Lord's Prayer.

> And forgive us our debts, as we forgive our debtors. And lead us not into temptation, but deliver us from evil: For thine is the kingdom, and the power, and the glory, forever. Amen. For if ye forgive men their trespasses, your heavenly Father will also forgive you. (Matt. 6:12–14)

Forgiveness always involves dealing with the negative emotions and thoughts toward a person because of an offense, whether real or perceived. Forgiveness is an internal decision, whereas the offense was external. Negative emotions toward a person are actually toward God and negatively affect our relationship with Him, as well as with other people. This is born out in the Bible.

> He that heareth you heareth me; and he that despiseth you despiseth me; and he that despiseth me despiseth him that sent me. (Luke 10:16)

The word translated *despiseth* is the Greek word *atheteo*. This word means to set aside, disesteem, cast off, disannul, despise, frustrate, or reject. In other words, it means just about any negative emotion. The same concept also appears in 1 Thessalonians 4:8.

A few years ago, my wife and I were in Washington D.C. and were watching a TV newscast. The reporter was interviewing a woman who had been beaten, raped, stabbed, and left for dead on the street a few weeks earlier. He asked her how she felt about the guy who did all this to her, and she replied that she had forgiven him. When she said that, the reporter was obviously awestruck by her response, and he asked how she could do that after all he had done to her. Her answer had to be from God because she said, "I had to give that man one day of my life, but I do not have to give him the rest of my life." This illustrates forgiveness of the offender and the freedom it gives the victim. When we do not forgive offenders, we give them control of our emotions.

There appear to be three major categories of forgiveness. The first I will discuss is what I choose to call divine forgiveness. This type of forgiveness can only be given by God and not by an individual, family, or church. Notice the primary steps involved in this type of forgiveness. First, the offender must initiate it; in other words, we have to realize that we need forgiveness and desire God's forgiveness. Second, the offender must confess wrongdoing. Thirdly, one must have a change of heart toward the wrongdoings. Then the person is forgiven, and the guilt of the offenses is removed.

> I acknowledged my sin unto thee, and mine iniquity have I not hid. I said, I will confess my transgressions unto the Lord; and thou forgavest the iniquity of my sin. Selah. (Ps. 32:5)

> And that repentance and remission of sins should be preached in his name among all nations, beginning at Jerusalem. (Luke 24:47)

If we confess our sins, he is faithful and just to forgive us our sins, and to cleanse us from all unrighteousness. (1 John 1:9)

A second type of forgiveness is what I call psychological forgiveness. This type of forgiveness can be defined as letting go of the desire for revenge and all negative feelings toward the offender, while extending grace to him or her. This type of forgiveness is "about letting go the bitterness that is eating us. By giving an unwarranted gift to someone who does not deserve it, we find paradoxically that is we, ourselves, who are freed from bondage" (Charlotte Witvliet). This type of forgiveness requires the victim rather than the offender to initiate the forgiveness process. This is the situation in Matthew 18:21–22, where Jesus tells Peter to forgive infinitely. This allows Peter to have peace of mind, and the offender does not control his emotions.

When we let go of our desire for revenge, we admit God is good to us and knows what is best for us. In other words, we let God take over and we exercise faith in Him. An interesting passage to consider in this regard is Romans 12:19.

Dearly beloved, avenge not yourselves, but rather give place unto wrath: for it is written, Vengeance is mine; *I will repay*, saith the Lord.

If we are willing to give up the desire for revenge, God will repay us for our pain. We are the ones who paid a price with our pain, and

He will make it up to us for that pain. Notice He does not say when or how He will repay us.

This type of forgiveness allows the victim to be in control of his or her emotions rather than the offender. Until we exercise this forgiveness, the offender is in control of our emotions. Forgiveness gives us peace of mind, and we avoid becoming bitter, but it does not restore the relationship. By this I mean that you probably will not have the same type of relationship with the offender that you had before the offense, unless the offender makes some changes so that you can trust him or her to not hurt you again.

You may wish to challenge me on this point, but please carefully consider it first. Sometimes we have to forgive God! You will probably think, "But God has not done anything wrong, so why should I forgive Him?" It is true that He has not done anything wrong, but on an emotional level we always blame God when things do not go the way we want them to. That is why we have to forgive Him, so we can have peace of mind. For instance, in Psalms 39 David is blaming God for all his trials, and then in Job 1:22 we see that Job did not "charge" God. In other words, Job did not blame God.

The third type forgiveness I choose to call reconciliatory forgiveness. This category of forgiveness is one in which the relationship is restored, or at least restoration is desired or attempted. Like ships, relationships sometimes sink. When one does sink, sometimes we are able to salvage all of it, and at other times we can only salvage part of it. The goal of this type forgiveness is reconciliation and restoration, but like judicial forgiveness, there are prerequisites. The major factor is that it requires repentance on the part of the offender in order for the relationship to be restored.

Some general guidelines for this forgiveness and total restoration of the relationship are as follows. Note that these guidelines are for the case where there was a real offense, not in the case where we simply feel that we were offended, but none was intended by the offender.

1. The offender must initiate the forgiveness process. This means the offender must desire and seek your forgiveness. In some cases, you may have to confront the offender and point out the offense. This is the case in Luke 17:3. "Take heed to yourselves: If thy brother trespass against thee, rebuke him; and if he repent, forgive him."

2. The offender must take full and total responsibility for the offense.

3. The offender must demonstrate appropriate remorse for the offense and the extent of damage done to victim.

4. The offender must establish adequate boundaries that demonstrate proper respect for the victim and provide future safety for the victim.

5. The offender must actively change behavior patterns that led to the offense.

6. It helps a lot if the offender also makes some kind of reparations for the damage or pain caused.

Remember that some relationships may never be fully restored, such as one in which there was sexual abuse. To try to fully restore the relationship in such a situation could subject the victim to even more abuse, even if it's only emotional. Sexual abuse is the deepest wound one can get. It goes all the way to the soul and requires spiritual "medicine" to be healed.

There are times when you have to seek someone's forgiveness. In doing this, you simple say something like, "What I did was wrong. Will you please forgive me?" Take full responsibility for what you did wrong. Try not to use the word *you* in relation to whatever happened. By this, I mean do not accuse others of any wrongdoing. You can use the word *you* in statements like "I must have really hurt you when I …." or," I really need you to forgive me for …"

There was a time I had to ask my mother's forgiveness. When I was about ten years old, my mother made my dad stop driving the car because his driving scared her. I got angry with my mother over that. As I grew up, I didn't realize that I was still angry with her. Some forty years later, it seemed that 95 percent of the arguments between my wife, Lois, and I occurred when we were in the car and I was driving. We finally began to explore why this occurred, and

I realized that I was still angry with my mom. I had to ask mom's forgiveness for having been angry with her. This is a delicate type situation, so note how it was handled.

I went to my mom and asked her forgiveness for having been angry with her. Naturally, she asked why I had been angry with her. This is the usual response when we ask forgiveness for having been angry with them or similar situations. In a way, it is a test to see if you are going to accuse them of some misbehavior. This is where and why you have to use extreme caution and careful wording. I said, "It doesn't really matter why I was angry. The important thing was about my having been angry with you, and that was wrong." She was not happy with that answer, but handling it this way does not require her to defend herself or why she did what she did.

Forgiveness for us is always a process and not a one-time deal. We have to wear out our emotions related to the offence. It begins with a conscious decision to forgive, and the more intense the wound, the longer it takes to complete the process.

The best approach that I have found to actually forgiving someone is a six-step process, which might have to be repeated many times depending on the severity of the offence. These steps involve verbalizing certain things and using hand motions to demonstrate them at the same time. Both are needed to increase the effectiveness of the process.

Step 1—Remember the pain and verbalize it while showing with your hands how painful it was (clenched fists, open hands, one hand slapping the other, etc.).

Step 2—Verbalize the feeling and hand each feeling back to God by stretching your hand and arm upward. Use hand motions to hand them up to God. An example might be, "Lord, here is my pain, my feeling unloved, my hurt feelings, my sadness."

Step 3—Verbally rage at the behavior while illustrating the amount of rage that you feel by using your hands. You might say things like, "It shouldn't have happened. It wasn't fair. I didn't deserve it." This step is often very difficult for Christian women because many of them have been taught not to express extreme anger.

Step 4—Now separate the person from what he or she did. Say, "I separate you from what you did," while using your hands and separating them to opposite sides, to show you are separating the two things.

Step 5—Verbalize that you forgive the person; again use your hands to illustrate that forgiveness. Verbalize how you can demonstrate that you forgive them. Never tell someone you forgave him or her unless the person asks for it. You might show it by putting flowers on a grave, by sending a card, or simply calling and tell the person you were thinking about him or her and wondered how he or she was doing. Then do what you verbalized. If you truly forgive people, you must serve them in some way like a greeting card, a phone call, a small gift, or praying for them.

Step 6—This is the icing on the cake. Verbalize how you can go even further in showing (to yourself) that you have forgiven people. Don't forget the hand motions. You might give them a gift or take them to lunch. It is going the extra mile. Then do whatever you just committed to do. You have completely forgiven them when you can honestly pray that God blesses them more than He blesses you. In addition, you may wish to do something nice for them.

God will probably give you many opportunities to learn how to forgive. Never miss such an opportunity. Problems arise to help us grow as God's children. He wants us to mature, just as we want our children to mature. The next chapter will illustrate another area in which God wants us to mature: in our way of thinking.

CHAPTER 13

EMOTIONS

IN OUR CULTURE and common usage, emotions and feelings are considered to be the same thing. Technically, feelings are physical sensations such a pin prick and the physical pain one feels from it. Emotions, on the other hand, are sensations originating from inside us. God has emotions, and He gave them to us. There are numerous mentions of God's emotions in scripture. The New Testament lists some twenty-seven different emotions that Christ had.

Emotions in and of themselves are not sin, but we have to be careful what we do with them. We should control them and not let them control us. In Romans 7, Paul says, "With the mind I serve the law of God but with the lusts/desires/emotions I serve the law of sin and death."

> *He that is* slow to anger *is* better than the mighty; and he that ruleth his spirit than he that taketh a city. (Prov. 16:32)

Emotions tend to add color to our lives. They are as much a part of us as our arms and legs. They are never right or wrong; they simply are. We all have them, but some folks express them more easily and more often than others. There are different ways that one can express emotions, such as facially, though motion (high-fives), vocally, musically, and more.

Emotions are real. That is, they exist, but they do not necessarily reflect reality. They are like a warning system or radar. They often provide an interpretation of what is going on in and around us. This interpretation can be reliable or unreliable—a misrepresentation, like a radar echo. A radar echo is something that occurs sometimes when using radar. The radar can display something that is not there, somewhat like a verbal echo across a valley. It "sounds like" someone is talking back at you, but no one is. Because our emotions interpret both correctly and incorrectly, we have to be very careful about trusting them. That is one reason God wants us to control our emotions rather than letting them control us.

Women tend to have more skill in handling their emotions than men in the areas of self-management, social awareness, and relationship management. Men and women are pretty equal in self-awareness. Men in our culture are usually taught to recognize just three emotions: mad, sad, and glad. Think about what we say to little boys when they get hurt, for instance: "Aw, just suck it up." "Don't be a crybaby." "Be a man and just take it." By doing that, we tend to stifle the boy from expressing his emotions. This training usually carries over into adulthood.

There are a number of things that can affect our emotions, such as the Holy Spirit, physical conditions, medications, our thinking, and our "beginnings." According to Galatians 5:22, certain emotions can be a barometer of the spirit; the expressions of joy and peace can indicate that we are living right, whereas their absence could indicate a fleshly walk (letting sin control us or a lack of trust in God's goodness to us).

> But the fruit of the Spirit is love, joy, peace, longsuffering, gentleness, goodness, faith. (Gal. 5:22)

Some general guidelines for dealing with your emotions in a healthy and godly way are as follows.

1. Thank God for the person or situation that triggered the emotion.

   > Giving thanks always for all things unto God and the Father in the name of our Lord Jesus Christ. (Eph. 5:20)

2. Ask God what He would have you learn from the situation.

3. Listen carefully for the answer.

4. Take six or eight deep breaths and hold them in for a count of four; then let out the breath very slowly while saying, "Relax."

5. Don't blame God for the situation.

6. Take a "trip in" (explained in the next couple of paragraphs).

I will use a model to describe how we operate as humans. Remember that models are used to help us to better understand how certain things function; they may not necessarily describe how things actually are as a model is not the actual thing.

Basically, the model is that we have a personal belief system (PBS), which is mostly formed by the age of ten. It is comprised of what we inherited, what we experienced, and what we were taught as children. In psychology, it is sometimes thought of as the subconscious (which is shaped by age, six according to Dr. David Stoop). The Bible calls it the heart (Prov. 4:23). I will refer to it as the PBS. It contains such beliefs (paradigms) as "life should be fair." Some beliefs are true, but others are not. Part of this model was suggested by Dr. James Mahoney.

> Keep thy heart with all diligence; for out of it are
> the issues of life. (Prov. 4:23)

The model is that the PBS gives rise to our thoughts, which in turn give rise to some emotions, which then result in our behavior.

Based on Ephesians 6:12, the PBS is the number one thing we wrestle with all of our lives. That verse says, "For we wrestle not against flesh and blood, but against principalities." The Greek word translated for *principalities* is *arche*. This Greek word is where we get our English word *archeology*, and it simply means "beginning." The same word is used in John 1:1. A corollary reference is 1 Peter 1:18. Even in the Old Testament, there is a passage (Num. 14:18) that conveys the same truth. These passages tell us that we have issues given to us by our forefathers with which we have to deal. These are lifelong struggles.

> For we wrestle not against flesh and blood but against principalities. (Eph. 6:12)

> In the beginning ... (John 1:1)

> Vain conversation received by tradition from your fathers. (1 Pet. 1:18)

> The Lord is longsuffering, and of great mercy, forgiving iniquity and transgression, and by no means clearing the guilty, *visiting the iniquity of the fathers upon the children* unto the third and fourth generation. (Num. 14:18)

The PBS determines for the most part how we think and what we think. Our thinking determines our emotions, which in turn determine our behavior—unless we overrule the emotions by making a conscious decision to do so.

Paul expresses this model in a reverse manner in Eph. 2:3 Among whom also we all had our conversation (behavior) in times past in the lusts (emotions) of our flesh, fulfilling the desires of the flesh and of the mind (thinking); and were by nature (PBS) the children of wrath, even as others. We find part of it in other verses.

> Keep thy heart with all diligence; for out of it are the issues of life. (Prov. 4:23)

> O generation of vipers, how can ye, being evil, speak good things? for out of the *abundance of the heart* the mouth speaketh. A good man out of the good *treasure of the heart* bringeth forth good things: and an evil man out of the evil treasure bringeth forth evil things. (Matt. 12:34–35)

> For *out of the heart* proceed evil thoughts, murders, adulteries, fornications, thefts, false witness, blasphemies. (Matt. 15:19)

> A good man out of the good *treasure of his heart* bringeth forth that which is good; and an evil man out of the evil treasure of his heart bringeth forth that which is evil: for of the *abundance of the heart* his mouth speaketh. (Luke 6:45)

Keep in mind that the signals from our five senses (hearing, seeing, touch, taste, and smell) all enter various lobes of the brain. The rational part of the brain is in the frontal cortex. That means the sensory signals enter the brain and travel through rest of the brain to the frontal lobe. So what is in the brain in these various lobes besides the sensory signals? There are a number of things in the middle of the brain, including memories and emotions. That means a lot of the time, things we sense can trigger emotions and memories from the past. This is much like radar echoes. This can cause us to want to react rather than respond in certain situations.

External events do not cause emotions. In other words, no one and no event can make you feel a certain way. Your emotions totally come from inside you, are all yours, and are a result from decisions you make either consciously or unconsciously. Very often your emotional reaction to an external event is due to your paradigms (beliefs). Remember, if it bugs you, it is your problem!

The first rule in dealing with a negative emotion (like depression, sadness, or anger) is to first thank God for the emotion and for whatever caused it. I will use a personal example. In 1999, I was diagnosed with a late stage of prostate cancer, and the actual words of the doctor were, "Go home and die." He felt that nothing could be done to correct the situation. That sort of message can give rise to all sorts of negative emotions. On the way back home from the doctor, I practiced what I preach. I thanked God for the diagnosis. Later, I decided to get a second opinion. That doctor performed surgery, and I am still alive and well in 2017.

How can we deal with our emotions in a healthy manner? After thanking God for them, I find it best to use a technique called "a trip in." When we have a behavior, emotion, or thought that we wish to correct or change, we need to take a trip in. Start with the behavior, emotion, or thought that is causing us difficulty and that we want to change or see why we have it.

If it is a behavior, we examine what emotion of ours gives rise to that behavior. Once we discover that emotion, we then examine what thought or thinking has caused that emotion. From there we go deeper, all the way to the PBS, to explore the underlying belief (paradigm) that gave rise to that thought. It may be a true belief or a false belief. By true I mean one that is accurate and is reality. A false belief is one in which we have a mistaken or inaccurate belief about reality.

Those things we wish to change have usually been based on some false belief. For example, if I believe in my PBS that I am not lovable, I will have a very hard time accepting love from others because I believe that I am unworthy of it. Whenever we encounter a false belief in our PBS, we need to replace it with a true belief. In this example, we could replace it with some belief like "God loves me, and that means I am lovable. I am a child of God and am worthy of being loved. If Christ died for me, I must be very valuable and lovable. As a born-again believer, I am already just like Christ, and that makes me very lovable."

> Herein is our love made perfect, that we may have
> boldness in the day of judgment: because as he is,
> so are we in this world. (1 John 4:17)

Let's look at some specific emotions and how the model can help us.

Anger is referred to in psychology as a secondary emotion. This means that there is at least one other emotion under it. Usually it is fear, and sometimes it's sadness. It always asks the question, "Why don't you love me?" One biblical example of this is found in Mark 3:5, where Christ was angry. This shows us that underneath His anger in this instance were sadness and grief. He also was asking the question, "Why don't you love me?"

> And when he had looked round about on them with anger, being grieved for the hardness of their hearts. (Mark 3:5)

It appears that each of us has at least one core fear. For women, it is normally insecurity—fear of not being heard and understood, not being valued, disconnection, abandonment, and losing love. Men's most common secret fear is that they are not really a man—not accepted as a man by other men, feeling controlled, fear of failure as a man, being run over by others, and loss of respect. That is one explanation for the macho mindset and behavior: men are trying to prove that they are really men.

These and other fears may be one reason why Christ said that He would never leave us or forsake us.

> Let your conversation be without covetousness; and be content with such things as ye have: for he hath said, I will never leave (physical) thee, nor forsake (emotional) thee. (Heb. 13:5)

We often think of women as being very emotional and men as being less emotional, at least in American culture. However, the opposite appears to be true. Various studies show men to be more reactive emotionally based on physiological responses (muscles, nerve, etc. measurements). The perception that they are not is partly due to the fact that women are much more verbally and facially expressive with their emotions, whereas most men are not. Men tend to express their emotions nonverbally by various physical motions such as high-fives and slaps on the back, and various sounds (grunts, groans, etc.). Men also often suppress their emotions (e.g., poker face).

As Christians, we should allow the Holy Spirit to control us, rather than be controlled by our emotions. Many of us have lived a number of years being controlled by our emotions, and upon salvation, there begins to be an internal conflict (Rom. 7:5, 15, 16, 25). Of half a million people tested, only 36 percent could accurately identify their emotions as they happen; 70 percent had trouble handling distress (otherwise known as worry or fear). It is difficult to resist the influence of our feelings, but it is necessary to do so if we are to live more rational, spirit-filled lives. Our emotions and what we choose to do with them must be evaluated against the truth of God's word.

Another secondary emotion is guilt. If you are guilty of something, that is one thing, but guilt feelings are altogether different and usually have resentment as an underlying emotion. Remember that negative feelings toward anyone are actually directed toward God (Luke 10:16, 1 Thess. 4:8). He is the one who brought, or allowed, that person or incident into your life as part of His good plan for your life (Jer. 29:11).

> For I know the thoughts that I think toward you, saith the Lord, thoughts of peace, and not of evil, to give you an expected end. (Jer. 29:11)

> He that heareth you heareth me; and he that despiseth you despiseth me; and he that despiseth me despiseth him that sent me. (Luke 10:16)

> He therefore that despiseth, despiseth not man, but God, who hath also given unto us his holy Spirit. (1 Thess. 4:8)

Feelings of low self-esteem usually result from basing our worth on our performance, which is often less than desired. The world system teaches us that we are worth only how much we can produce.

> Not of works, lest any man should boast. (Eph. 2:9)

This passage shows that it is not about our performance (works) but about who we are. How do you think Jeremiah would have felt about himself if he had looked only at the result of his preaching for some thirty years, where no one listened to him?

Depression stems from either the physiological condition of our body or from our emotions. If it is caused by some physiological condition, you may need some medication or medical treatment. Antidepressant medication is not a solution for emotional depression, but it helps get you to a somewhat normal state so that you can better deal with it. Depression is often a learned behavior from our parents or others. They may have taught us (intentionally or otherwise) to react this way when things do not go the way we wanted them to go.

If your depression is learned, you can unlearn it. Some things you can do to unlearn it are to rename it laziness, tell at least six people how you feel (but do not say what triggered it), and do something physical for someone else (like wash a car or mow the lawn).

When it comes to depression, the National Institute of Health found that baby Boomers (those born between 1946 and 1964) had ten times more depression than any prior generation. A group of psychologists studied this phenomenon and decided that it was the result of letting the people out of relationships too easily, one example being no-fault divorces.

CHAPTER 14

ANGER

ANGER IS AN attribute of God and is the most damaging of all emotions. It is probably the most misunderstood (and certainly the most misused) emotion. It is the greatest deterrent to intimacy and the second most often mentioned emotion in scripture (about 450 times, of which 350 refer to God's anger). Love is the most mentioned (remember, real love is not an emotion but a conscious decision and action).

> God judgeth the righteous, and God is angry with the wicked every day. (Ps. 7:11)

Psychology understands anger is a secondary emotion, which means there is one or more emotions underneath it. Most of the time the underlying primary emotion is fear, and sometimes it is sadness. One biblical example of this is found when Jesus had looked round about on them with anger (orge), being grieved for the hardness of their hearts … In this example, the emotion under Jesus's anger apparently was sadness and grief.

And when he had looked round about on them with anger, being grieved for the hardness of their hearts, he saith unto the man, Stretch forth thine hand. And he stretched it out: and his hand was restored whole as the other. (Mark 3:5)

It is the most deceiving of all emotions. It puts you in your weakest position because you are making yourself the victim! It feels like you are strong, but actually you have chosen to be your weakest because it lets the abuser control your emotions. Anger is an emotion that gives Satan an opportunity to use and abuse us. Anger is one's normal reaction to personal boundaries being violated, and it always asks the question, "Why don't you love me?"

There are two primary types of anger: aggression and passive aggression. Passive aggression is normally used by those who strongly resist ugly displays of anger. Some of these behaviors are a lack of neatness, tardiness, laziness, procrastination, and withdrawal (silence, pouting, sulking). This approach to anger is usually chosen by those who have a strong need to control with minimum vulnerability. It is recognized by suppressed anger, blaming self, dependent, denial, avoiding conflict, and over-responsibility.

Aggression includes rage, short tempers, intimidation, blame, criticism, griping, bickering, sarcasm and sometimes violence. The person who chooses this mode of expression usually develops a strong insensitivity to the needs of others. Those using this mode usually have a lot of personal insecurity.

Anger is self-generated. It can be triggered by external events, but it still is generated from within the individual. There are three primary ways in which an individual generates anger: physiologically/ emotionally, cognitively, or behaviorally. No one can "make you angry"—it is always a choice you make.

We love to hang on to our anger because it makes us feel like we are in control. Being in control was part of Eve's temptation ("be as gods," Gen. 3:5). Why do we want to be in control? There are several possibilities, some of which are: it gives us a sense of value and importance, an attempt to evade responsibility, we might be afraid of something, an inability to properly communicate, habit, we don't recognize we are angry, and we don't believe in God's goodness to us. Sometimes it is used as a substitute for love. It can become an addiction due to the adrenaline rush it produces.

When we feel threatened, there is a two-stage reaction within the body. The first occurs within three seconds, and the body is aroused. The second occurs about ten seconds later, when adrenaline and noradrenalin are released into the body. The current physiological condition of the body (i.e., recently fed, tired, ill) determines the magnitude of the effect of these hormones on the body. This is why one can overreact to a situation when one is tired.

The effect of these chemicals on the body creates what is commonly known as the flight or fight syndrome. They prepare the body for vigorous physical activity by shutting down stomach activity, shifting the concentration of blood in the body, causing the capillaries near the skin's surface to retreat in case of wounding, and changing the breathing pattern to short, rapid breaths.

If the chemicals are released into the body and no vigorous activity takes place, there can be some very toxic effects. The chemicals settle some place in the body, and where they settle varies from person to person. Their toxic effects can cause stomach and bowel problems, lower back pain, or aching neck or shoulders. This may be one reason why God tells us to not let the sun go down on our wrath (Eph. 4:26). When we go to bed angry, we usually get up the next morning even angrier.

A study lasting 25 years and using the records of 225 physicians found that hostile (i.e., angry) men are six times more likely to experience coronary heart disease than non-hostile men. Very often we call it stress, but in reality we are simply angry because things are not going our way.

So what is God's purpose in giving us the emotion of anger? We are commanded by God to "be ye angry and sin not" (Eph. 4:26). Anger is given to us to give us the energy to accomplish God's purposes, which is sometimes part of maturing us.

> Be ye angry, and sin not: let not the sun go down
> upon your wrath. (Eph. 4:26)

Did you notice the "don't let the sun go down upon your wrath" part of that verse? In other words, do not ever go to bed angry. What can you do about your anger? You have to learn to control it rather than letting it control you. The first two commandments in learning to properly deal with anger are to shut up and to walk away. We have to be careful about walking away when we are dealing with our spouses. They can feel abandoned if we don't say something like, "I'll be back shortly. I just need to cool off before we continue our discussion."

We also need to realize and remember that "hurt people hurt people." When people hurt your feelings, they are normally in pain and want you to know that. It provides a good opportunity for you to minister to them by asking them what they are feeling. It is best to discuss the feelings rather than what caused the feelings; we cannot change the facts, but we can change the feelings.

Other steps in learning to control your anger are to thank God for the person and what they did (Eph. 5:20) or did not do, forgive the offender, and ask God what He wants you to learn from the situation.

> For if ye *forgive men their trespasses*, your heavenly Father will also forgive you: But if ye forgive not men their trespasses, neither will your Father forgive your trespasses. (Matt. 6:14–15)

> *Giving thanks always for all things* unto God and the Father in the name of our Lord Jesus Christ. (Eph. 5:20)

Have you been doing this? You will do things God's way or the hard way. The choice is yours.

CHAPTER **15**

FEAR

PROBABLY NOTHING MAKES more of an impression on our brains than fear. When we are facing danger, whether real or perceived, our minds and bodies go into a survival mode. Sometimes this is called fight or flight. Physiologically, we mobilize for vigorous physical activity. The adrenal glands release more adrenalin and cortisol into the bloodstream, which speeds up the heart rate and breathing; more blood flows to the large muscle areas; the blood changes so as to coagulate faster in order to minimize blood loss if one gets wounded.

The major theme in the media today is that of fear—fear of the failing economy, terrorists, various natural disasters, or what will happen if a certain candidate is elected. Families are faced with more challenges in today's culture. For instance, "An estimated 40 million Americans suffer from some form of anxiety disorder" (National Institute of Mental Health, 2008).

What are you afraid of? Maybe you are afraid of the flu, flying, losing your job, failure, making a mistake, people not liking you, or losing your spouse, health, or savings.

The Bible tells us over and over again (125 times) to not be afraid, but to trust God and His love and protection. That does not mean we will not have some tribulation—in fact, we are promised that we *will* have tribulation (John 16:33). It is part of our maturing process (Rom. 5:3). David gives us an example in Psalm 131:2 about "quieting ourselves." This example shows us that it can be done, it is a learning process, and it is intentional—a sign of maturing. If even a child can do it, why can't you?

> These things I have spoken unto you, that in me ye might have peace. *In the world ye shall have tribulation*: but be of good cheer; I have overcome the world. (John 16:33)

> And not only so, but we glory in tribulations also: knowing that *tribulation worketh patience*. (Rom. 5:3)

> Surely *I have behaved and quieted myself*, as a child that is weaned of his mother: my soul is even as a weaned child. (Ps. 131:2)

Here are some fear facts.

1. It is unavoidable, unless you are dead or unconscious.

2. It is a normal part of life.

3. It is not a sin.

4. It is usually only temporary.

5. It can be a source of motivation for you to make changes.

6. It's used by God to grow us in faith.

7. It's used by Satan to try to defeat us.

8. It is the emotion giving rise to our anger most of the time

Are you afraid of tribulation? It can be pretty scary to consider. Have you stilled your soul? Do you know how to still your soul (quiet yourself)?

> Confirming the souls of the disciples, and exhorting them to continue in the faith, and that we must *through much tribulation* enter into the kingdom of God. (Acts 14:22)

We are going to have difficult situations in life; that is part of our inheritance as a believer, and that is how we really enter into the real kingdom of God—by submitting to Him and to His decisions, and by trusting Him. We talk a lot about our being part of the kingdom, but do we really let God rule our lives and depend on Him to protect us?

When we encounter a difficult situation, we normally experience some fear. "What am I going to do? How will I survive? How would God have me respond?"

When you are confused, fearful, or hurting, God has you in a place where He can grow you. God does His best work with us when we are in the "waiting room." It makes a real difference on how you choose to view your situation. You can view the situation from the present (temporal) perspective, or from the eternal perspective. The temporal perspective says, "I have to do it." The eternal perspective says, "God has a good purpose in this for me, and He is going to help me through this."

The present/temporal perspective is focused on the flesh: "I have to solve it. I have to do it. What can I do? How can I fix it?" The eternal perspective is focused on faith: (Thank you, Lord, for this situation. I need your help to get through this: "I can't do it without you. I accept this as being for my best interest."

Which would help you more? Which does God want you to use?

Notice Psalm 23:4. Are you in a valley? What is the shadow in your life? Notice that it is the "shadow of death." It is *not* death, but you may feel like it is going to kill you. But that is a feeling and not necessarily a fact. Usually the shadow represents depression, sadness, or some similar emotion. How will you choose to get out of your valley? David is not going to set up camp in the valley; rather, he decides to walk through the valley, holding on to God's rod and staff.

> Yea, though I walk through the valley of the shadow
> of death, I will fear no evil: for thou art with me;
> thy rod and thy staff they comfort me. (Ps. 23:4)

> Blessed are those whose strength is in you, who have set their hearts on <u>pilgrimage.</u> As they pass through the Valley of Baca, they make it a place of springs (a source of satisfaction); the autumn rains also cover it with pools. They go from strength to strength, till each appears before God in Zion. (Ps. 84:5–7)

> Baca means to weep. It comes from the Hebrew word, bakah (baw-kaw'); a primitive root; to weep; generally to bemoan.

Baca is made into a place of springs by those that pass through it. There is nothing better on a hot day when you're thirsty and weary than to drink water from a cool mountain spring. It refreshes and renews. It gives you a second wind to continue your journey. Those who commit themselves to a pilgrimage with God will experience the Valley of Baca. But in the midst of Baca, they will discover that in this valley, they will also drink from a very special spring that refreshes with a different kind of living water.

Each Valley of Baca will result in a new spiritual spring from which you can drink. It is handmade just for you by God. But know this: God intends that it will be used to provide a refreshing drink for others you will encounter who are also on their pilgrimage.

> Who comforteth us *in all our tribulation,* that we may be able to comfort them which are in any trouble, by the comfort wherewith we ourselves are comforted of God. (2 Cor. 1:4)

In order to walk out of your valley, you have to make a conscious decision to do so by holding the hand of Jesus. Is that how you are going to walk out of your valley?

> For which cause we faint not; but though our outward man perish, yet the inward *man* is renewed day by day. For *our light affliction, which is but for a moment, worketh for us* a far more exceeding and eternal weight (abundance) of glory; While we look not at the things which are seen, but at the things which are not seen: for the things which are seen are temporal; but the things which are not seen are eternal. (2 Cor. 4:16–18)

Do you let God comfort you in your tribulation? When you do, then you can experience peace in your particular valley.

> Now faith is the substance of things hoped for, the evidence of things not seen. (Heb. 11:1)

> There is no fear in love; but *perfect love casteth out fear:* because fear hath torment. He that feareth is not made perfect in love. (1 John 4:18)

Are you willing to trust God in your situation? If not, why not? If you don't trust God in your situation, you are teaching your folks to not trust God in their situations. Is that what you really want to do?

CHAPTER 16

PERSONAL SEX

YOU MIGHT WONDER why such a subject is included in a book on ministerial stress. There are several reasons for its inclusion. One is that our culture is very focused on sex. Another is that sexual sins affect our very spirits, and there are folks out there who want you to fail sexually and who actively work to achieve that.

Where did you learn about sex? From your parents? From kids you grew up with? From movies or TV? Is your sex life all that you thought it would be? What are your myths about sex? What if your ideas about sex were all wrong? Is your sex life what you anticipated? What would improve it?

Have you ever heard a sermon on sex? Have you ever brought a sermon or lesson on sex? Are you afraid to do so? Why? Don't the people need to know what God says about it? So when are you going to bring such a sermon or lesson? The sooner, the better.

What is sex all about? It is about a meaningful physical part of a loving, committed relationship. A real, total relationship involves the body, soul, and spirit, and sex involves all of these. A lot of times in church, we hear much said about agape love, like that is the best and all there is to it. But in reality, one cannot demonstrate agape love without eros love. Eros love means using the physical body, and in order to express agape love, we need to use our bodies. Eros is *not* just about sex.

Great sex is a special gift to those who have love as a priority in life. Why do you think God relegated sex to marriage? There are several reasons, one of which is because He did not want it separate from a loving, committed relationship. Without love and commitment, sex becomes a craving that is never satisfied and usually results in some form of sexual addiction.

> Marriage is honourable in all, *and the bed undefiled*:
> but whoremongers and adulterers God will judge.
> (Heb. 13:4)

When you truly experience sexual love the way God meant for it to be, you are learning true love. Remember that love is all about giving, not getting.

Sin wants us to separate sex from love. Often the husband is focused on his sex drive, whereas the wife is starved for affection. Real love doesn't allow this to happen, but it is a learning process. This is one reason why sexual frequency usually decreases with length of relationship and depth of love: we focus on giving more than getting. When the two are separated, sex becomes a craving, an addiction; one's body or lust is in control, rather than the spirit. Sexual love is much more than a brief period of ecstasy. Sex is everything that results from the act of sex: family, church, and society.

Regular sex is good for your health. Dr. Harold Bloomfield, in *The Power of Five*, shows that regular sex maintains higher estrogen levels in women (better bones and cardiovascular health) and higher testosterone levels in men (greater energy and strength).

Your sex drive (libido) is normally determined about three weeks before birth by your mother's body chemistry. I'm not sure, but this may be the original motivation for all the mother-in-law jokes. Maybe this is why men have so much difficulty with their mothers-in-law. One's libido can be affected by porn input or by abuse. Additionally, certain medications, drugs, alcohol, physical conditions, and emotional states affect it. Your most important sex organ is between your ears: your brain.

The person with the lower sex drive determines the frequency of sex. Women don't feel the need for sex until their need for a sense of feeling loved is fulfilled. Love is more important than sex to them. Men tend to get much of their emotional fulfillment during sex. Men need sex to begin to feel (as opposed to fighting dragons all day with emotions shut down). For example, the skin of women is ten times more sensitive than men's. A person's acceptance of his or her own body is crucial. This is a critical element in self-acceptance. You don't really accept others until you accept yourself.

The big myth fostered by magazines and other media is that it's all about climax. Climax is the end, not the substance in an intense sexual encounter; the maximum duration of intense intercourse is about three minutes.

When it comes to sexual arousal, men are commonly aroused by sight, and women are aroused by touch.

An interesting related scripture is 1 Corinthians 7:1. "Now concerning the things whereof ye wrote unto me: It is good for a man not to touch a woman." Men can often take only three minutes to be fully aroused, but it is not unusual for it to take women forty-five minutes to be fully aroused. Or as Gary Smalley says, "Men are like microwave ovens, while women are like crockpots."

For most people, there is a difference in the sexual experience. For men, it is primarily physical, an event; his objective is normally orgasm, and there can be a hidden agenda such as confirming his masculinity. In many cultures other than ours, sexual relations follow, or at least accompany, achievement of manhood. In our culture, it is becoming the primary way to achieve manhood.

For women, the sexual experience is mostly emotional. She rarely separates feeling loved from sex, and it may be a reflection of her life as a whole. Her primary objective is closeness and love, and orgasm is only one of many steps to the objective—not the main one. She does want her femininity affirmed, but sex does not define it. She rarely feels the freedom to express her sexual needs to her husband (because of his fragile sexual ego).

A common concept is that men trade love for sex; they "take" sex. Women trade sex for love, and they "give" sex.

Biblical perspective tells us it is intended to be a part of physical intimacy (1 Cor. 7:4). Note that it doesn't say "the genitals" belong to each other—it's the whole body. So what does the body mean? Implicit in this is that the whole body is meant to be enjoyed, as a physical sharing. I am not talking about kinky sex, but I do mean such things as backrubs and cuddling.

> The wife hath not power of her own body, but the husband: and likewise also the husband hath not power of his own body, but the wife. (1 Cor. 7:4)

The bottom line is that God intended sex to be fun and enjoyable. The next few verses give you some tips on how to do this.

> Let thy fountain be blessed: and rejoice (Hebrew = samach) with the wife of thy youth. (Prov. 5:18)

> > The simple definition of "samach" is "to enjoy" or "to have fun."

Sex is a debt that we owe our spouses.

> Let the husband render unto the wife *due benevolence*
> *(Greek = eunoia):* and likewise also the wife unto
> the husband. The word "eunoia" means; kindness;
> *euphem. conjugal duty*:—benevolence, good will.
> (1 Cor. 7:3)

There is only one biblical reason given to not have sex, and that is because you are having a time of prayer and fasting. When it is over, you should have sex.

> *Defraud ye not one the other*, except it be with consent
> for a time, that ye may give yourselves to fasting and
> prayer; and *come together again*, that Satan tempt
> you not for your incontinency. (1 Cor. 7:5)

An overall perspective begins with foreplay, which is where it's at rather than climax.

> Let her be as the loving hind and pleasant roe; let
> her breasts satisfy thee at all times; and be thou
> ravished always with her love. (Prov. 5;19)

This perspective allows the total experience to last as long as you desire. Once there's a signal for actual intercourse to begin, that says physical intimacy is about to end. Climax is the signal that physical intimacy has ended. If you are married, do you know what the signal for intercourse from your spouse is?

There is a definite link between female's climax and trust. In a loving relationship, the man takes the woman to the very edge emotionally. For her to climax, she has to trust that the man will be careful with her emotions. A real-life example that I once dealt with is one in which a couple had been married some twenty years, and she had never climaxed. When she decided to trust her husband with her emotions, she totally changed. I ran into her husband about two months later, and he said, "She is about to kill me. She has become a nymphomaniac."

Your sex life tells the story of your real relationship. In other words, your sex life is an excellent measure of the health of the relationship. If the sex life is not satisfying to both parties, the partners need to make some changes in how they relate to each other.

Here are some practical tips on how to improve your sexual relationship. The first thing to consider is who gives the signal for penetration. If it is the man, the woman may not be fully aroused, and she may feel that her feelings are being ignored; she may feel he is being selfish. The next point to consider is the signal. It doesn't matter much what the signal is, as long as both agree on what it is. Sex is best when both can climax about the same time. That is one reason for her to be fully aroused prior to penetration.

Climax is the sign that the sex is over, but the physical relationship can continue by hugging each other after sex. God did not call us to have godly marriages; He called us to be godly spouses. Among other things, that means you are to be very loving and giving in the relationship.

Another aspect of personal sex is that of masturbation. If a person is single and masturbates, there is a high risk of becoming addicted to it. This is one of the most difficult addictions to break. Even if one is married, the potential of addiction exists, along with establishing an emotional atmosphere that will affect your children in a negative manner. If you are married, your body (including the sex organs) belongs to your spouse (1 Cor. 7:4), so you are not free to do with it as you will—you need to have his or her permission.

CHAPTER 17

THEOLOGY OF SEX

SEXUALITY IS ONE of the most misunderstood and frightening subjects around. Have you ever heard a sermon on sex? With some 40 percent of babies born in America out of wedlock and over 50 percent of our young women between the ages of fourteen and nineteen years old having a sexually transmitted disease, why don't we hear more from the church about sex? Why do we let our kids learn about sex on the street rather than in church? Did one of your parents ever have a sex talk with you?

There are several reasons why, not the least of which is that sexuality is intimately connected to spirituality. Another one is that it involves intimacy and nakedness. Still another factor is the lack of knowledge about it.

Think about it: where did sin first show up? It manifested itself in the genitals, and that is why Adam and Eve made aprons to cover that area.

> And the eyes of them both were opened, and
> they knew that they were naked; and they sewed
> fig leaves together, and made themselves aprons.
> (Gen. 3:7)

Along with that, consider what happened when God then came to the Garden: they hid themselves. God asked Adam why he was hiding, and he said because he was naked. Then God asked, "Who told you that you were naked?" The Bible does not state exactly how Adam replied, but it appears that he took his eyes off Eve and put them on himself. He hid not only from God but also from Eve.

Another bit of evidence that spirituality and sexuality are connected is found in the covenant God made with Abraham.

> And he gave him the covenant of circumcision: and
> so Abraham begat Isaac, and circumcised him the
> eighth day; and Isaac begat Jacob; and Jacob begat
> the twelve patriarchs. (Acts 7:8)

> Once again, the connection between spirituality
> and sexuality is evident.

Why is fornication a sin against one's own body, but drunkenness, overeating, and more are not identified as such? Because there is something special about our sexuality. Our sexuality affects our holiness, whereas the other things do not.

> Flee fornication. Every sin that a man doeth is
> without the body; but he that committeth fornication
> sinneth against his own body. (1 Cor. 6:18)

For this is the will of God, [even] your sanctification, that ye should abstain from fornication. (1 Thess. 4:3)

Dr. M. Scot Peck makes the observation that "sexuality and spirituality sleep in the same bed and you cannot awaken one without awakening the other." I would like to explore this relationship with you as a possible explanation of why sexuality is such a mystery to us.

Basically, we are spiritual beings. Therefore anything that affects our spirituality affects us as a person.

herewith bless we God, even the Father; and therewith curse we men, which are *made after the similitude of God*. (James 3:9)

God is a Spirit: and they that worship him must worship him in spirit and in truth. (John 4:24)

We were made to be in relationship with others. This is evident when God stated that it was not good for man to be alone, so he made Eve.

And the Lord God said, It is not good that the man should be alone; I will make him an help meet for him. (Gen. 2:18)

Spirituality is measured by (and determined by) our relationships. The kind of spirituality we have is determined by our relationship with God. The kind of relationships we have with others is affected by our spirituality.

It is God who separated the woman from the man, and it is He who brings them back into oneness through marriage. Sexuality differentiates between man and woman; it is also the element that unites them (1 Cor. 6:16).

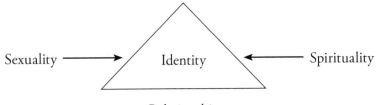

So God created man in his [own] image, in the image of God created he him; male and female created he them. (Gen. 1:27)

Note that the word "create" is used **three times** in this verse. Perhaps this has something to do with the triune Godhead. Perhaps it has something to do with three parts to one's identity (spirituality, relationship, and sexuality).

Note that it is Adam who is created, having both male (zakhar = male) and female (neqebhah = female, to perforate) elements. This might imply androgyny is perfection.

Note that being in God's own image involved sexuality (male and female). Does this mean that God is sexual? If sexuality was not very important, why did God mention it as part of being in His image?

Maybe that is why Satan tries so hard to corrupt the image of God, by attacking so many people through sex.

Sin showed up first in our sexuality.

> And the eyes of them both were opened, and they knew that they [were] naked; and they sewed fig leaves together, and made themselves aprons. And they heard the voice of the LORD God walking in the garden in the cool of the day: and Adam and his wife hid themselves from the presence of the LORD God amongst the trees of the garden. (Gen. 3:7–8)

Why hide? They were ashamed. The first noticeable effect of sin was shame. Shame was related to sexuality. Adam apparently didn't see himself prior to the fall, or he was content with what he saw.

We are addicts or slaves to looking at ourselves through other people's eyes. We are often more concerned about how others see us then how God sees us. Sex has to do with relationships and to the degree that we are dysfunctional in our sexuality, to the same degree we are dysfunctional in our relationships. God clothed Adam and Eve out of compassion for their pain in shame.

Nudity (i.e., the nudist movement) appears to be an attempt to return to Eden without going through God. All cultures agree on what nakedness is, but not all agree on what fully clothed is. Nakedness is a sense of or feeling of being exposed, vulnerable, and open. These are the very feelings that we have to overcome to develop real relationships

All family, church, community, and social concepts arise out of sex. It is only after creation of male and female that human society becomes a possibility. The first place sin showed up was related to the genitals. Why?

a.   The source of life had been polluted.

b.   Mankind's spirituality had been affected, and it showed up in the physical area first.

c.   Mankind tends to focus on the outward appearance rather than the inner being.

d.   Mankind relates through gender/sexuality (male to male, male to female, female to female).

e.   Sexuality and spirituality are intimately connected.

Sexual sins appear to be in a special category apart from other sins.

> For this cause shall a man leave his father and mother, and shall be joined unto his wife, and they two shall be one flesh. This is a great mystery: but I speak concerning Christ and the church. Just what is the "mystery" here? Perhaps it is a type of "spiritual sexual union." (Eph. 5:31–32)

Why is adultery so awful? It demanded the death penalty under Mosaic law, but fornication did not. Why does it head the list of sins of the flesh?

> For this, Thou shalt not commit adultery, Thou shalt not kill, Thou shalt not steal, Thou shalt not bear false witness, Thou shalt not covet; and if [there be] any other commandment, it is briefly comprehended in this saying, namely, Thou shalt love thy neighbour as thyself. (Rom. 13:9)

> Now the works of the flesh are manifest, which are [these]; Adultery, fornication, uncleanness, lasciviousness. (Gal. 5:19)

One reason is that it destroys or distorts God's picture of the relationship between Christ and the church, which is pictured in marriage.

Sexual abuse affects our identity. Cloe Madanes, the nation's leading expert on treating sexual abuse, states, "Sexual abuse is a spiritual wound and requires spiritual medicine to heal." Even secular therapists see the connection between spirituality and sexuality. With so much evidence of the relationship between spirituality and sexuality, and with such a need for a proper sex education need in this country, why aren't we hearing God's perspective from the church?

Are you going to be part of the problem or part of the solution?

CHAPTER 18

SOME EVERYDAY DOS AND DON'TS

YOUR FAMILY IS your first ministry. Always put them ahead of your church ministry.

> For if a man know not how to rule his own house, how shall he take care of the church of God? (1 Tim. 3:5)

If God has called you into the ministry, He will use you for His glory. You may not see the results right away. Don't worry about it. If you keep lifting up Christ in your sermons, lessons, and life, God will produce real results. Too many churches and ministers forget to keep Christ in the forefront, and yet that is what ministry is really all about.

Stay in touch with God. By this, I mean listen to what God tells you and then do it. He may use the Bible, the Holy Spirit, some person, or your own brain (common sense).

Prayer should probably be more listening to God than talking to Him. Don't get me wrong: He wants you to communicate with Him. Communication is a two-way street.

Never talk negatively about one church member to another church member. You will be surprised how fast the discussion will get back to the person talked about if you do not follow this rule.

Encourage the folks in your ministry to serve. In many churches, the people expect the minister to do all the work. They are missing many blessings by not serving.

God holds you responsible for setting the right example for the people.

Instead of trying to raise money from the people for a ministry project, consider "lowering it" from God. God has enough money to pay cash for everything that He wants.

If and when you hire a staff person, you normally get what you pay for. A good staff person usually pays for himself within a year.

All of our distress stems from the conflict of our personal agenda with that of God's agenda.

"The opposite of truth is not error, it is unrighteousness."
—John D. Morgan

The price of godliness is pain and suffering.

"God is in the process of raising children, not students!" —John D. Morgan

"What is God's will for my life? Answer—It's not my life!" —Louie Giglio

Until you learn to rest and relax, you haven't found God's will for your life. Man needs a Sabbath, and that includes ministers.

Do you want your ministry to be a voice or an echo?

God doesn't have any problems with our failures; it is our strengths that He has to deal with.

Pressure-driven people never take time for spiritual refreshment— just the opposite of priority driven people.

When you discover that you are riding a dead horse, dismount.

The real blessing of God's word lies not in learning more, but in applying to your life what you already know.

Pearls are the only precious stones that result from suffering.

Character is doing what is right, on purpose.

Are you trusting God or your money to take care of you?

Then Peter began to say unto him, Lo, we have left all, and have followed thee. And Jesus answered and said, Verily I say unto you, There is no man that hath left house, or brethren, or sisters, or father, or mother, or wife, or children, or lands, for my sake, and the gospel's, But he shall receive an hundredfold now in this time, houses, and brethren, and sisters, and mothers, and children, and lands, with persecutions; and in the world to come eternal life. (Mark 10:28–30)

CHAPTER 19

SERVING IN MINISTRY, NOT MISERY

HERE ARE SOME guidelines for a more effective ministry. These guidelines repeat the previous chapter to some small degree but are more focused on ministry effectiveness.

Remember that real ministry is God's job, and the results are His responsibility. Do not focus on the numbers.

The best, and only correct way, to deal with ministerial stress is God's way. Thank God for it (Eph. 5:20).

Christ promised us trials, and each trial is an opportunity for us to grow in our faith and to better equip us to be able to minister to others.

Stress is designed to build your faith when you respond to it God's way. Distress is bad for you and damages your physical and emotional health.

In stressful situations, we usually try to change the cause. The correct approach is to change the effect of stress on us. We best do this by thanking God for the stress and asking Him what we should learn or change in ourselves as a result of that stress.

> *Giving thanks always for all things* unto God and the Father in the name of our Lord Jesus Christ. (Eph. 5:20)

> Enter into his gates with thanksgiving, and into his courts with praise: be thankful unto him, and bless his name. For the Lord is good; his mercy is everlasting; and his truth endureth to all generations. (Ps. 100:4)

Let the situation change you rather than always trying to change the situation.

Do not take criticism personally. It is usually an issue between the critic and God, or a family issue.

Do not strive to grow your ministry numerically; that is God's job, and you are not equipped to do His job.

> And I say also unto thee, That thou art Peter, and upon this rock I will build my church; and the gates of hell shall not prevail against it. (Matt. 16:18)

Have a weekly Sabbath, a time and place away from church ministry responsibilities. It is a time to rest and admire God's creation.

If an issue cannot be resolved rationally, it is an emotional or spiritual problem.

You are not to try to do all the work of the ministry by yourself. You are to equip the people to do the work of the ministry.

> And he gave some, apostles; and some, prophets; and some, evangelists; and some, pastors and teachers; For the perfecting (complete furnishing) of the saints, for the work (deed, doing, labour, work) of the ministry, for the edifying of the body of Christ. (Eph. 4:11–12)

If you do all the work and have all the answers, then you are teaching your folks that they do not need God, just you.

It is extremely helpful to have one or two mentors, such as ministers who have experience in successfully dealing with stress.

We need to learn to quiet ourselves when we get upset. This is done by trusting God and His goodness—and with lots of practice.

> And that ye study to be quiet, and to do your own business, and to work with your own hands, as we commanded you. (1 Thess. 4:11)

> But let it be the hidden man of the heart, in that which is not corruptible, even the ornament of a meek and quiet spirit, which is in the sight of God of great price. (1 Pet. 3:3)

Not that I speak in respect of want: for I have
learned, in whatsoever state I am, therewith to be
content. (Phil. 4:11)

For I know the thoughts that I think toward you,
saith the Lord, thoughts of peace, and not of evil,
to give you an expected end. (Jer. 29:11)

There shall no evil happen to the just: but the
wicked shall be filled with mischief. (Prov. 12:21)

When you follow these guidelines and God's directions, you will
serve much more effectively in ministry and not in misery!

An excellent verse to keep in mind to help you grow in ministry
and not misery is Psalm 23:6.

Surely goodness and mercy shall follow me all the
days of my life: and I will dwell in the house of the
Lord for ever.

How could David write this? Look at some of his trials. His father
overlooked him at times, he had to fight a giant, he married Saul's
daughter, Saul had the army out trying to kill him, one son raped his
daughter, and one son tried to take his throne away. The key word
here in this passage is *follow*. We normally have to get through a
stressful situation and grow in faith before we can look back and see
God's goodness and mercy in that situation. We normally cannot
see God's goodness when we are in the midst of pain and trials. It is
only afterward that we can see God's goodness and mercy.

You are most vulnerable to temptations when you are emotionally exhausted.

If you are a senior pastor with a staff, it is wise to have and use a personnel committee for hiring and firing. This is especially true when a staff person requires discipline or discharge.

Never talk about one church member with another church member. Instead, utilize one of your mentors.

Teach your folks how God says to do church.

Consider "worry" as an acronym:

* **W** = Wait a minute. "take several deep breaths" (Jam. 1:4; Matt. 6:34)

* **O** = Opportunity. "to grow, to trust God" (Gal. 6:10)

* **R** = Rejoice. "Rejoice in the Lord always" (Phil. 4:4)

* **R** = Remain calm. "let God handle the situation His way" (John 15:4)

* **Y** = You can and do choose your emotions. You choose whether you will trust God or not. Whom you will serve? God wants you to control your emotions, not let them control you.

CHAPTER **20**

UNDERSTANDING MY GIFTEDNESS

MINISTERS ARE MOST effective when they operate out of their giftedness. Operating outside your giftedness is stressful and not very effective.

So just what is your giftedness? Do you truly know what it is? How do you know? Among other things, it involves emotional self-awareness, which means knowing what your emotions are and recognizing how your emotions affect your ministry. That requires making an accurate self-assessment; knowing your inner resources, strengths and weaknesses, and abilities and limits; and having an objective sense of your self-worth and capabilities.

One way to find out what your giftedness is to see what God says.

> And he gave some, apostles; and some, prophets; and some, evangelists; and some, pastors and teachers. (Eph. 4:11)

Having then gifts differing according to the grace that is given to us, whether prophecy, let us prophesy according to the proportion of faith; Or ministry, let us wait on our ministering: or he that teacheth, on teaching; Or he that exhorteth, on exhortation: he that giveth, let him do it with simplicity; he that ruleth, with diligence; he that sheweth mercy, with cheerfulness. (Rom. 12:6–8)

From these lists, the office (position) gifts are an apostle, a prophet, an evangelist, a pastor, and a teacher. They're followed by seven more spiritual gifts, some of which are related to the offices: prophecy, ministry, teaching, exhortation, giving, ruling (administration), and mercy.

If you are a pastor, do you have a real passion for shepherding the congregation, or do you simply enjoy standing and preaching to them? If you have the gift of pastoring, you will have the passion for the people and their needs.

If you are a teacher, is your passion for studying, learning, and teaching? If not, you are not operating out of your giftedness. Another clue to look for is that of seeing real changes in the lives of your people through your teaching.

Perhaps your giftedness is that of an evangelist. You will be passionate about telling folks about Christ and how to be saved, whether from the pulpit or out on the street. If this is your gift, do not get bound up in the numbers that actually accept Christ. It is your job to tell them how to get saved, and it's the Holy Spirit's job to draw them in.

The giftedness of ministry is being able to meet the people's real needs with a passion for doing that, whether the office is that of pastor, senior adult minister, youth minister, teacher, music director, or whatever. This means meeting spiritual, emotional, and other needs of the people.

If you do not really love and enjoy what you are doing, you probably are not working out of your giftedness.

The gift of exhortation allows one to encourage and build up people. This is especially true if they are hurting for any reason.

The gift of giving involves loving enough to give money, oneself, and time to others.

The gift of ruling is that of administration. This person is one who knows how and when to assign tasks to others, and who can organize people, places, and things. This gift allows the one with it to focus on the main thing and keep things on track to meet that goal.

Effective leaders keep their disruptive emotions in check. They are able to empathize, listen, and value differences. One way to think about it is, "People don't care how much you know until they know you care about them."

There are some spiritual gifts tests that you can take to get a good idea of which of the seven spiritual gifts you have (Rom. 12:6–8).

You should control your emotions and not let them control you.

CONCLUSION

THIS MAY BE the final chapter of this book, but it is certainly not the conclusion or final chapter of your ministry. I covered what I consider the major areas of challenges you can expect to face in ministry, but there are many that I have not covered. Regardless of that, God is still in control and will carry you through if you depend upon Him. I do wish to remind you of a few things.

Ministry is the most difficult and stressful vocation in the world. It is also the most rewarding when you obey God, especially when you can see lives changed for the better and for eternity.

Your responsibility is to proclaim the truth of God's word in your life, your family, and your ministry. You are not responsible for the results; God is responsible for the results. You plant the seeds, and God produces the fruit that He desires. That may not always be what you desire. We only teach that, or anything else, by example.

If God called you into the ministry, He will use you in one way or another to minister to others until the day He calls you home. There really is no retirement from ministry; God's callings are without revocation.

Every problem or difficult situation you encounter is an opportunity for you to build your faith. Each time you hit a bump in the road, remember to thank God for the bump, and ask Him what He wants you to learn or change.

Your family's welfare is your primary ministry. Always put your family's welfare ahead of the ministry in your priorities.

A major thing you will wrestle with all your life is what you inherited from your forefathers, what you experienced, and what you were taught growing up. I really like what an old cartoon character, Pogo, used to say: "I have found the enemy, and it is me." Much of what we encounter and have to deal with involves our own emotions and points of view.

The problem is never the problem. It is usually just a symptom or metaphor for the real problem.

Hurt people hurt people. You will encounter folks who will criticize you over nothing. As a general rule, they are hurting and want you to know that, so they hurt you. It is usually an opportunity for you to minister to them. Do not take it personally, even though they mean it that way.

Christ said that He would build the church. It is not your job to do that. Your job in ministry is to live a life that is an example of how God wants us to live. We only teach by example.

Forgiveness is always for the person, not the deed or lack thereof.

Please do not lead your people or church into debt. Nowhere in the Bible do God's people borrow money. I know it is tempting to borrow so that you can hurry up and do or get certain things. God has enough money to pay cash for anything He wants. Teach the people to give to God and not to a necessity. Pray down money rather than raising it. If God wants it, He will supply the money without borrowing.

Men, if you are married, God will usually speak to you more through your wife than any other way. Women, and also men, there is wisdom in a multitude of counselors.

Many of us are more comfortable with suffering than with joy; we enjoy being a martyr. We like to think that we are "suffering for Jesus."

Many (if not most) ministers feel like they have to be and look serious all the time, but God says laughter does good like a medicine. Keep a smile on your face most of the time. "Most of the men of the cloth I have seen looked like they hold down a night job at the local mortuary" (Charles Swindoll, *Laugh Again*, p. 13). God tells us to rejoice over and over again, so start doing it.

TOPICAL INDEX